Cat-alogue

A BOOK OF CAT NAMES

Jenny Linford

Thorsons
An Imprint of HarperCollins*Publishers*

For Spicioli, Tensingh and Paris –
three wonderful cats

Thorsons
An Imprint of HarperCollins*Publishers*
77–85 Fulham Palace Road
Hammersmith, London W6 8JB
1160 Battery Street
San Francisco, California 94111–1213

Published by Thorsons 1995

10 9 8 7 6 5 4 3 2 1

Jenny Linford asserts the moral right to
be identified as the author of this work

A catalogue record for this book
is available from the British Library

ISBN 0 7225 3207 5

Printed in Great Britain by Woolnough Bookbinding Limited,
Irthlingborough, Northamptonshire

Introduction

Bringing home a tiny new kitten is one of life's great joys but brings with it a unique problem. What should this engaging little creature be called? Do you know its character well enough to decide on a name? What name would you feel happy about calling out in front of the neighbours? Will it, and you, be teased if you choose something unsuitable? As the poet T. S. Eliot so perceptively wrote: 'The naming of cats is a difficult matter'...

When we got our first joint kitten it took weeks of discussion and even argument before a name could be agreed upon.

'We've got a lovely kitten,' I told friends excitedly.

'Ooh, what's it called?' was the inevitable question.

'Well, we haven't quite decided yet... We're trying to choose,' was my lame response.

In the end our cat was called Paris – a name prompted by the city rather than Greek mythology. It was a name plucked out of the air after days of trying out different ones and failing to agree; a name which miraculously we both liked and were prepared to use. Sheer exhaustion was probably a key factor in our decision.

This book has been devised to help other kitten owners before they are reduced to similar straits.

ABRACADABRA A magical name for cats of either sex, inspired by an ancient incantation, famously used by witches and wizards.

ABYSSINIA A majestic African name, suitable for cats of either sex, inspired by the north-eastern African country now known as Ethiopia. The name is, of course, especially appropriate for Abyssinian cats, short-haired cats descended from one exported to the UK from Abyssinia in the nineteenth century.

ACAPULCO An especially appropriate name for fun-loving male cats, inspired by the popular Mexican beach resort, known as the Mexican Riviera.

ACHILLES A suitable name for warrior tom-cats. In Greek mythology Achilles was the great Greek hero in the Trojan War whose only vulnerable spot was his heel.

1

ADONIS An appropriate name for dazzlingly handsome tom-cats. In Greek mythology Adonis was a young Cypriot, beloved by Aphrodite because of his great beauty.

AÏDA An operatic name for vocal female felines. The name is inspired by Verdi's tragic opera in which the eponymous heroine Aïda, an Ethiopian princess enslaved in Egypt, dies to save her people.

AJAX A good name for large tough tom-cats, inspired by the legendary Greek hero who was great both in stature and in courage. In Homer's *Iliad* he fights Hector in single combat.

ALABAMA An American name for male cats. Alabama is a south-eastern state in the USA on the Gulf of Mexico.

ALBINA A feminine name appropriate for white cats. The name comes from the Latin *albus*, meaning 'white', and was introduced into Britain from Italy in the seventeenth century.

ALEXANDER A noble, masculine cat name, after the heroic Macedonian king. While in his twenties

Alexander the Great conquered most of Asia Minor, Syria, Egypt, Babylon and Persia.

ALFA   A stylish car-inspired name for male or female cats. In Italy, Alfa cars are prized for their stylishness and speed.

ALFRED   A venerable masculine English name, derived from Old English and meaning 'wise man'. Famous bearers of the name include the heroic King of Wessex Alfred the Great and the Swedish chemist Alfred Nobel, who initiated the Nobel Prizes.

ALI   A snappy name for truly tough tom-cats, after the champion boxer Muhammad Ali. His famous catch-phrase was that he 'could dance like a butterfly and sting like a bee'.

ALICE   The elegant name of a dainty white-and-grey cat of my acquaintance. Despite her gentle appearance she has a true flair for hunting, with victims including budgerigars and guinea pigs.

AMARETTO   An Italian name for spirited cats of either sex. Amaretto is a popular Italian liqueur derived from almonds.

AMAZON An appropriate name for strong and warlike female felines. In Greek mythology Amazons were female warriors who lived in Pontus and were trained for hunting and war.

AMBER An elegant name for yellow-eyed female felines. Amber is a translucent or opaque yellow fossil resin hardened over centuries and used in jewellery.

AMBROSE A male name, highly popular in medieval times and suitable for dignified felines. St Ambrose was a great teacher of Christianity, while Ambrosius Aurelianus was a medieval warrior.

AMORE A rhythmic Italian name for beloved and lovable cats of either sex. *Amore* is Italian for 'love'.

AMORETTE A dainty feminine name for adored felines. *Amorette* means 'beloved' in French.

AMSTRAD A snappy, techno-name for contemporary tomcats with a penchant for keyboards. The name is inspired by the popular personal computers found in many households.

ANCHOVY An appropriate name for diminutive, fish-loving cats of either sex. Anchovies are small herring-like fish usually eaten salted and especially popular in Mediterranean cuisine.

ANGOSTURA An exotic name for female felines, inspired by Angostura bitters, an aromatic blend of herbs and spices used to add flavour to food and drink.

ANGUS A fine upstanding Scots name for tom-cats. Angus comes from the Gaelic name Aonghus, which means 'unique choice'.

APOLLO An appropriate name for golden-furred, sunny-natured tom-cats. In Greek mythology Apollo was the handsome god of the sun, famous for his physical beauty and musical gifts.

APPLE A fruit-inspired name for cats of either sex. Apples have an ancient history, being famously mentioned in the biblical Book of Genesis as well as in Greek mythology. Today they are viewed as typically English fruit.

APRICOT A fruit-inspired name for ginger cats of either sex. Orange-fleshed apricots are prized in Middle

Eastern cookery and add an exotic sweetness to sweet and savoury dishes.

AQUARIUS A zodiac-inspired name for water-loving cats born between 21 January and 18 February.

ARABIA An exotic name for cats of either sex. Arabia, a Middle Eastern peninsula, was home to ancient civilizations and was dominated by the Turks from the sixteenth century to WWI.

ARABICA For coffee-coloured cats of either sex. Arabica is the most widely-grown coffee tree, producing the highest quality beans.

ARAGON An elegant Spanish name for dashing male cats. Aragon was a medieval kingdom in north-eastern Spain, united with Castile through royal marriage in 1469.

ARAMIS An elegant French name for refined but coura-geous tom-cats. In Dumas's famous swash-buckling novel *The Three Musketeers*, Aramis is the dandy musketeer of the trio.

ARCHIBALD An old-fashioned, aristocratic name for male cats, originally from the German for 'very bold'. Famous examples include Archibald Leach, the real name of handsome, debonair actor Cary Grant.

ARCHIMEDES An appropriate name for thoughtful male cats who enjoy sitting in bathtubs. Archimedes was a Greek mathematician and inventor, famous for shouting 'Eureka!' when he discovered the Archimedes principle while taking a bath.

ARIA An operatic name for vocal female felines. Arias are solo songs with instrumental accompaniment.

ARISTO A Greek name for aristocratic male cats. In Greek *aristos* means 'best', hence 'aristocracy', meaning government by the best of the group.

ARISTOTLE A name for thoughtful male cats. Aristotle was an influential ancient Greek philosopher and scientist, who studied under Plato and taught Alexander the Great.

ARLETTY A feminine name, after the beautiful, enigmatic French actress. In Carne's poetic film *Les Enfants du Paradis* she appears as Garance, the epitome of Sphinx-like femininity.

ARMANI   A designer name for handsome felines. Italian
         fashion designer Giorgio Armani's clothes are
         internationally famous for their elegance.

ARMSTRONG   A jazz name for vocal tom-cats. Louis Armstrong
            was a black jazz trumpeter and singer from New
            Orleans, famous for his gravelly voice and superb
            trumpet playing.

ARNIE   A tough name for macho cats, after film hunk
        Arnie Schwarzenegger, famous for his belligerent
        screen persona. The name Arnold is derived from
        Old German Arinwald, from *arin*, meaning 'eagle',
        and *vald* meaning 'power'.

ARSENAL   A football-inspired name for competitive tom-cats.
          Arsenal, the highly successful and famous north
          London football team, commands a huge, loyal
          following of fans.

ARTEMIS   A very appropriate name for predatory female
          cats. In Greek mythology Artemis was the
          beautiful and ruthless goddess of the hunt, also
          associated with the moon.

ARTHUR   A noble name for handsome male cats. King

Arthur was the legendary British king, founder of Camelot and the Knights of the Round Table, celebrated in medieval romances.

ASCOT   For aristocratic and fleet-footed felines of either sex. Ascot racecourse in Berkshire is famous for Royal Ascot, a major racing and social event, traditionally opened by the sovereign.

ASLAN   For majestic, golden-furred, leonine tom-cats. In C. S. Lewis's Narnia books, beloved by generations of children, Aslan is the awe-inspiring, god-like great lion.

ASPARAGUS   A vegetable-inspired name for cats of either sex. Prized as a luxury, asparagus was also famous in Roman times for its aphrodisiac qualities.

ASSAM   An Indian name for cats of either sex. Assam is a famous tea-growing state of north-eastern India, where the high rainfall supports the plantations.

ATALANTA   An appropriate name for swift-footed female felines. In Greek mythology, Atalanta was a famous huntress, who promised to marry any man who could outrun her. She was defeated by

Hippomenes, who distracted her during the race by dropping a golden apple in her path.

ATHENS A classic Greek name for male cats. In ancient times Athens was the leading Greek city state, famous in European culture as a democracy.

ATHOS A French name for tough tom-cats. Athos was a rugged musketeer in Dumas' *The Three Musketeers*.

AUDREY A feminine cat name inspired by the beautiful actress Audrey Hepburn. With her gamine looks and expressive eyes, she starred in classic films such as *Roman Holiday* and *Breakfast at Tiffany's*.

AUGUSTUS An imperial name for dominating male cats. Augustus, adopted son of Julius Caesar and the first Roman Emperor, secured and expanded the then disintegrating Roman Empire.

AVA A glamorous female name, after film star Ava Gardner. Her dark Spanish looks meant she often starred as exotic beauties, as in *Pandora and the Flying Dutchman*.

AVOCADO A fruit-inspired name for cats of either sex.

Avocado pears, with their soft, scoopable pale green flesh, are high in vitamins and attributed with aphrodisiac powers.

AZTEC   An ancient name for cats of either sex. The Aztec Indians of central and southern Mexico had an advanced and elaborate civilization until overthrown by the Spanish conquistadors in the sixteenth century.

AZURE   A beautiful name for blue-eyed cats of either sex. Azure means 'sky blue' or 'cloudless sky' and is from the Perisna *lazward*, the name for the semi-precious blue stone lapis lazuli.

BABBAGE For ingenious male cats. Charles Babbage was the notable British mathematician and inventor who conceived the idea of a mechanical computer.

BABS The endearing, feminine diminutive of Barbara.

BACCHUS For fun-loving male cats who enjoy life. Bacchus was the Greek god of wine and pleasure, famous for drunken Bacchanalia, riotous festivals in his honour.

BAGHEERA An appropriate name for handsome black tom-cats. Bagheera was the name of the noble and sleek black panther in Kipling's *Jungle Book*.

BALI A tropical name for cats of either sex. Bali is an Indonesian island which epitomizes the idea of a tropical paradise island and is a famous holiday destination.

BALTHAZAR   An appropriate name for regal tom-cats. Balthazar was the name of one of the three Magi who brought gifts to the baby Jesus.

BALZAC   A literary name for down-to-earth tom-cats. Balzac was a nineteenth-century French novelist, who developed literary realism in novels like *Le Père Goriot* and *La Cousine Bette*.

BAMBOO   A name for cats of either sex, evocative of the Far East. Bamboo is a graceful tropical and subtropical giant grass, especially prevalent in South East Asia. An especially appropriate name for cats of Eastern origins, such as Siamese or Burmese.

BANDIT   A good name for rogue male cats with a flair for thieving.

BANGKOK   An exotically Eastern name. Bangkok, also known as 'the City of Angels', is the capital of Thailand. The name therefore is particularly appropriate for Siamese cats.

BARBARY   A dashing name for piratical male cats. Barbary is a region in North Africa which was notorious for its pirates.

13

BARRYMORE   A thespian name for dramatic male cats. The Barrymores were a famous theatrical family, made up of thespian siblings Lionel, Ethel and John.

BARYSHNIKOV   A Russian name for graceful male tom-cats. Mikhail Baryshnikov is a leading Soviet-born ballet dancer, famous for his physical ability and technique.

BASIL   An appropriate name for regal male cats. Basil comes from the Greek *basilon*, meaning 'royal'. Famous Basils include St Basil the Great, the second-century Bishop of Caesarea, and Basil Brush, the jovial puppet fox.

BEANO   A humorous male name inspired by the classic children's comic. The word *beano* means 'bean-feast', that is, a celebration or merry time.

BEATRICE   A female Latin name meaning 'bearer of happiness'. Beatrice was the name of Dante's great love and also of Shakespeare's witty character in *Much Ado About Nothing*.

BEAU   For good-looking male cats, from the French for 'handsome'. Beau Brummell was the name of a famous eighteenth-century dandy, close friend of the Prince Regent.

BEETHOVEN   A musical name for classically good-looking male cats, inspired by Ludwig van Beethoven, the great German composer.

BEHEMOUTH   A literary name for large black cats. In Russian writer Mikhail Bulgakov's satiric novel *The Master and Margherita*, Behemouth is a devilish walking and talking cat 'black as soot and with luxuriant cavalry officer whiskers'.

BELLA   An appropriate name for beautiful female felines. *Bella* means 'beautiful' in Italian.

BELLADONNA   A name evocative of witches and magic, especially suitable for female black cats. Belladonna is another name for deadly nightshade, associated with spells.

BELLE   An appropriate name for attractive female cats. *Belle* means 'beautiful' in French.

15

BENEDICK A suitable name for dashing bachelor cats. In Shakespeare's *Much Ado About Nothing*, Benedick is a confirmed bachelor until he is beguiled into wooing and marrying the sharp-tongued Beatrice.

BENGAL For tiger-striped cats of either sex. Bengal is a north-eastern region of the Indian subcontinent, divided among India and Bangladesh, and traditionally an area where tigers can be found.

BENJAMIN A male name, often abbreviated to 'Benjie'. Benjamin is a Hebrew name meaning 'Son of my right hand'. Famous Benjamins include Victorian Prime Minister Benjamin Disraeli and twentieth-century British composer Benjamin Britten.

BENNIE Suitable for loyal, slightly dim tom-cats. Bennie was Top Cat's faithful sidekick in *Top Cat*, the TV cartoon series about a smart alleycat.

BEOWULF A suitable name for heroic warrior cats. In Norse mythology Beowulf defeats the fearful monster Grendel.

BERTIE An endearing, down-to-earth male name. P. G. Wodehouse fans will be familiar with the simple-minded Bertie Wooster, whose life is guided by his discreetly intelligent valet Jeeves.

BERYL A mineral-inspired name for female cats. Aquamarine and emeralds are both gem varieties of beryl, so the name is particularly appropriate for green- and blue-eyed cats.

BETHLEHEM A religious name for serene female cats. Bethlehem, near Jerusalem, is the birthplace of Jesus Christ.

BIANCO An appropriate name for white male cats. *Bianco* is Italian for 'white'; *bianca* is the female version.

BIBA Suitable for slinky, large-eyed female felines, this name is evocative of the 1960s, when Biba make-up was glamorously popular.

BIBI An endearing name for playful cats of either sex which derives from the French *beaubelot*, meaning 'bauble' or 'toy'.

BILKO A faintly comic name, good for clowning cats. Sergeant Bilko is a popular humorous character from the eponymous TV series.

BILLIE   A musical name for female cats, after Billie Holiday, the great black jazz singer, who was also known as Lady Day, and performed with Count Basie and Artie Shaw.

BILLY   A boyish name for adventurous tom-cats. Billy the Kid was a famous gun-slinging outlaw in the American West.

BINGO   A name for lucky black cats of either sex. Bingo, a gambling game developed in the 1880s from the children's game of Lotto, is still popular today.

BLACK JACK   With its liquorice associations, this is an appropriate name for a black cat. It was given to a cat at the British Museum.

BLACKIE   A straightforward no-nonsense name given to black cats of either sex.

BLANCO   An appropriate name for white tom-cats. *Blanco* is Spanish for 'white', with *blanca* being the female version.

BLONDIN   For acrobatic male cats. Charles Blondin was a nineteenth-century French acrobat and tightrope walker, famous for walking across a tightrope suspended over the Niagara Falls.

BLOOMSBURY A literary name for London tom-cats. Bloomsbury was the name given to a group of English writers and artists active in the 1910s and 1920s, including Virginia Woolf, E. M. Forster and Lytton Strachey.

BLUE A name particularly appropriate for smokey-blue pedigree cats.

BOADICEA For combative, queenly female felines. Boadicea was the courageous Queen of the Iceni, who rebelled against the Romans, sacking Colchester, London and St Albans.

BOBCAT For tough tom-cats with a penchant for snow. The bobcat is a short-tailed wild cat, closely resembling the lynx, found in North America.

BOCCACCIO An Italian name for rumbustious tom-cats. Giovanni Boccaccio was a fourteenth-century Italian writer and poet, author of the *Decameron*, a bawdy collection of 100 tales.

BODMIN Inspired by the mysterious Beast of Bodmin, the
name given to a handsome big black cat living in
Somerset.

BOGART A Hollywood-inspired name for rugged tom-cats.
Humphrey Bogart came to epitomize the tough
screen hero in films such as *To Have and Have Not*,
Casablanca and *The Big Sleep*.

BOLIVAR For independent-minded tough tom-cats. Simon Bolivar was a South American soldier, known as 'the Liberator', who campaigned for political independence for Latin America from 1807 to 1830.

BOLSHOI A ballet-inspired name for graceful cats of either sex. The Bolshoi is the principal Russian ballet company, based at Moscow's Bolshoi theatre.

BONGO A music-inspired name for rhythmic tom-cats. Bongo drums are a pair of small drums held between the knees and played with fingers.

BONSAI An oriental name for small cats of either sex. Bonsai trees are ordinary shrubs or trees that are developed into miniatures, a technique originally practised in China over 700 years ago, then perfected by the Japanese.

BOOTS A name for a black cat with elegant white 'boots'.

BORAGE A herbal name for cats of either sex. Borage, with its small blue flowers, is used in herbal remedies and beverages.

BORGIA   For cunning cats of either sex. The Borgias were a notorious fifteenth-century family, infamous for their political scheming and plotting.

BORIS   A Russian name for aggressive tom-cats. The name comes from the Slavonic *borotj*, meaning 'to fight'.

BOTTICELLI   An artistic name for beautiful male cats. Botticelli was the Italian Renaissance artist who painted 'The Birth of Venus' and 'Primavera'.

BOURBON   A drink-inspired name for mellow cats of either sex. Bourbon, an American malt, is famed for its smoothness.

BRAINS   The perfect name for a super-intelligent cat. Fish, most cats' favourite food, is reputedly good for the small grey cells.

BRANDO   The perfect name for tough tom-cats, inspired by rugged film star Marlon Brando, the glowering hero of classic films including *On the Waterfront* and *The Wild One*.

BRANDY   A spirit-inspired name for golden-coloured cats of either sex. Brandy, distilled from fermented grape juice, is traditionally enjoyed as an after dinner drink.

BRAZIL A tropical name for large male cats. This huge country covers almost half the area of South America.

BRUBECK A jazz name for cool tom-cats. The American jazz pianist Dave Brubeck studied composition with Arnold Schönberg and formed his own quartet in 1951.

BRUMMELL A classic name for elegant tom-cats. Beau Brummell was a famous eighteenth-century dandy and leader of fashionable society.

BRUNO For tough, muscular tom-cats. Boxer Frank Bruno became European heavyweight champion in 1985.

BRUTUS A Roman name for fearless male cats. Brutus was the Roman soldier who joined the conspiracy to murder Julius Caesar.

BRYONY A plant-inspired name for black or white female

cats with a penchant for climbing. Black and white bryony are both climbing plants.

BUBBLES A humorous name, suitable for dizzy felines of either sex. Bubbles was the name of the dim PR girl in the popular TV series *Absolutely Fabulous*.

BUCKINGHAM A masculine name with regal overtones. The Duke of Buckingham was a leading courtier under James I, while Buckingham Palace is the London residence of the sovereign.

BUDDHA A serene name for cats of either sex, particularly suitable for oriental cats such as Burmese or Siamese. In sixth-century India, Gautama Siddhartha, who became the Buddha, founded a monotheistic religion which has over 500 million followers around the world.

BURGUNDY A French name for cats of either sex. Burgundy, a region of France, was where the French writer Colette, a noted cat-lover, was born.

BURMA An exotic name for either male or female cats, particularly appropriate for Burmese. Burma is a South East Asian country on the Bay of Bengal.

BURTON A name for handsome male cats, inspired by Welsh actor Richard Burton. With his noble good looks and deep voice he achieved success in films like *Look Back in Anger* and was famously married to actress Elizabeth Taylor.

BUSTOPHER JONES A name from *Old Possum's Book of Practical Cats*. Bustopher Jones was T. S. Eliot's sleek, black 'cat about town' with white spats on his feet, at home in the clubs of St James.

BUTTERCUP A floral name for rural, golden-furred female cats. Buttercups, with their distinctive bright yellow flowers, are found in English meadows and fields.

BUTTONS A domestic name for bright-eyed cats of either sex. Buttons was the name given to liveried page boys because of the buttons on their jackets.

BYRON A poetic name for dashing tom-cats. George Gordon Byron was the famous poet much lionized by London society and notorious for his romantic lifestyle.

CACHAO   A musical Cuban name for tom-cats, inspired by
            the veteran Cuban musician Cachao.

CACTUS   For cats with especially prickly claws. Cactus
            plants are notorious for their sharp defensive
            spikes.

CAIRO   An Egyptian name for cats of either sex. Cairo,
            the capital of Egypt, is the largest city in Africa.

CALLIOPE   For vocal female felines. In Greek mythology
            Calliope, whose name comes from the Greek for
            'beautiful-voiced', was the muse of eloquence.

CALYPSO   A music-inspired name for rhythmic cats. A
            calypso is a West Indian song, very popular
            throughout the Caribbean.

CAMBRIDGE   A respectable English name for wise tom-cats.

The town of Cambridge is famous for its ancient
university.

CAMPBELL   A Scottish name for rugged male cats. The
Campbells form an ancient Scottish clan.

CANCER   A zodiac-inspired name for sharp-clawed cats
born between 21 June and 22 July.

CANDY   An appropriate name for sweet-natured cats of
either sex. Candy is another name for sweets.

CAPPUCCINO   A chic Italian name for coffee-coloured cats of
either sex. Cappuccino is the classic frothy coffee
served in Italian bars and now very popular in
England.

CAPRICORN   A zodiac-inspired name for agile cats born
between 23 December and 20 January.

CARA   An affectionate name for beloved female cats. In
Italian *cara* means 'dear'.

CARAMEL   A name for sweet, golden-furred cats, inspired by
the toffee-flavoured sweet.

CARAVAGGIO   An artistic name for sinuous male cats.
Caravaggio was an Italian Baroque painter noted
for the dramatic contrast between light and dark
in his work.

CARBONNEL   An unusual cat name, given to a noble cat in
Barbara Sleigh's children's book *The Kingdom of
Carbonnel*.

CARMEN   An operatic name for dramatic, beautiful female
cats. In Bizet's eponymous opera, Carmen is a
passionate woman whose turbulent love life
results in her death.

CARTER   The Unstoppable Sex Machine – a rock band-
inspired name a friend of mine gave his large,
lazy tom-cat.

CARUSO   The operatic name given to writer Edward Gosse's
stately cat. Caruso was the famous Italian tenor.

CARY   A Hollywood name for debonair tom-cats,
inspired by suave actor Cary Grant, star of films
like *Suspicion* and *Notorious*.

CASBAH   An exotic name for cats of either sex, casbah is

the name given to the Arabic quarter of cities in North Africa.

CASHMERE For soft, fluffy cats of either sex. Cashmere wool is the fine wool from Kashmir goats, valued for its softness.

CASSANDRA A legendary name for prophetic female cats. Cassandra, the daughter of King Priam of Troy who had prophetic powers, foresaw the destruction of Troy but her prophecies were disbelieved by those she warned.

CASSAVA A plant-inspired name for female cats. Its edible, starchy tubers are a staple food in many parts of the tropics.

CAT A fundamental but much-loved name given to many felines.

CATHERINE An appropriate name for imperial female felines. Catherine was an eighteenth-century Empress of Russia who oversaw the expansion of Russia's territories.

CATO A Roman name for statesman-like male cats.

Cato the Elder was a Roman elder who wrote the first history of Rome.

CAVOUR An Italian name for shrewd tom-cats. Cavour was the nineteenth-century Italian statesman who engineered the unification of Italy.

CAYENNE For hot-tempered cats of either sex. Cayenne pepper is a hot red chilli pepper from a plant native to Cayenne in French Guyana.

CEFALU An Italianate name, given to the endearing feline hero of Rosemary Harris's children's book *The Moon in the Cloud*.

CHAGALL An artistic name for dreamy male cats. The Russian artist Marc Chagall was famous for his dreamlike paintings, such as 'Me and the Village'.

CHAMPAGNE For glamorous cats of either sex. Champagne is the famous sparkling wine from the Champagne region in France, evocative of the high life.

CHANTILLY A French name for dainty female felines. Chantilly is a town in France once famous for its lace-making.

CHAPLIN   A film-derived name for comic black tom-cats.
           Charlie Chaplin was the famous film star whose
           humorous portrayal of a pathetic tramp won him
           international audiences.

CHARCOAL   An artistic name for black cats of either sex.
           Charcoal, made from burnt wood, is used by
           artists to draw with.

CHARLES   A dignified name for male cats. Charles was a
           popular name in medieval times and acquired
           royal associations over the centuries, Prince
           Charles being a current example.

CHARLESTON   An American name for rhythmic male cats. The
             Charleston, named after the town of Charleston
             in South Carolina, became a popular ballroom
             dance in the 1920s.

CHARLOTTE   An old-fashioned French female name which is
            the female version of Charles and was popular-
            ized in England by Queen Charlotte, wife of
            George III.

CHARLTON   A football-inspired name for rugged tom-cats.
           Footballer Bobby Charlton played for England

106 times and was a member of the England team that won the 1966 World Cup, along with his brother Jack, who later became a successful manager of the Republic of Ireland.

CHAT   A classic cat name, particularly popular with Francophiles. *Chat* is French for 'cat'.

CHEETAH   For fleet-footed cats of either sex. The cheetah, a large African feline, is the fastest mammal in the world, sprinting up to 70 mph (110 kph).

CHELSEA   A smart London name for cats of either sex. A chic residential district in London, Chelsea is noted for its artistic and literary associations.

CHÉRI   From the French for 'dear', suitable for beloved cats (*Cherie* is the female version). *Chéri* is a novel by French author Colette, a great cat-lover.

CHESHIRE CAT   For good-natured male cats. The Cheshire Cat was the cat with a huge grin created by Lewis Carroll in *Alice in Wonderland*.

CHEVALIER   A distinguished French name for elegant, impeccably-mannered male cats. Maurice Chevalier was a French singer and actor who starred in films including *Love in the Afternoon* and *Gigi*.

CHIANG MAI A Thai name, perfect for Siamese cats of either sex. Chiang Mai is a town in north-west Thailand famous for its picturesque temples.

CHIANTI An Italian name for male cats. Chianti is a region of Tuscany famous for its fine wines.

CHILLI For hot-tempered cats of either sex. Chillies are small hot members of the capsicum family, used in cooking.

CHINA An oriental name for cats of either sex. China is the great East Asian country with one of the world's oldest civilizations.

CHINOOK A Native American name for fish-loving male cats. The Chinook were a Native American people living along the north-west Pacific Coast who were salmon fishers and traders.

CHIVES A herb-inspired name for cats of either sex. Chives, a member of the onion family, are a popular herb, used as a seasoning.

CHLOË A pastoral Greek name, especially appropriate for rural female felines. The name comes from the Greek *kloe*, meaning 'green' and was the name of the goddess of young crops.

CHRISTMAS A festive name for cats of either sex, especially those brought home at this time of year.

CHUTNEY A food-inspired name for cats of either sex. Chutneys are flavoured mixtures of fruit or vegetables, used to accompany foods such as cold meats or cheese.

CINDERS A feminine name from the fairy-tale *Cinderella*. The name comes from the French *cendres*, meaning 'ashes', as the down-trodden Cinderella is made to sweep the ashes from the hearth.

CINNAMON A spice-inspired name for brown cats. Cinnamon is a fragrant bark from a member of the laurel family, used to flavour both sweet and savoury dishes.

CLARENCE An affectionate name given to a gentle cross-eyed lion in the popular 1960s TV series *Daktari*.

CLAUDIUS   An imperial name for male cats. Claudius, from the Latin *claudius*, meaning 'limping', was the name of the physically disabled Roman Emperor Claudius I, hero of Robert Graves's book *I Claudius*.

CLEOPATRA   An elegant name for captivating female felines. The name comes from Cleopatra, the beautiful and intelligent Queen of Egypt who entranced both Julius Caesar and Mark Antony.

CLINT   A Hollywood name for long, lean, macho cats. Clint Eastwood is the tough, gun-slinging star of Westerns like *A Few Dollars More* and *The Good, the Bad and the Ugly*.

CLOUD   A evocative name for white and grey cats, inspired by clouds in the sky.

CLOVE   A spice-inspired name for cats of either sex. Cloves are aromatic flower heads, native to South East Asia and valued for their flavouring and medical properties.

COBALT   For blue-eyed cats of either sex. Cobalt blue is a deep blue pigment containing cobalt.

COCOA   An appropriate name for chocolate-brown cats.
Chocolate is made from the fermented, dried pulp
of cocoa seeds.

COGNAC   A mellow name for cats of either sex. Cognac is
the name of a famous brandy made in and
around the town of Cognac in western France.

COLETTE   An elegant feminine name in homage to the
French author. Colette, author of the best-selling
Claudine novels, adored cats and wrote about
them beautifully in many of her novels and
stories.

COLOMBIA   A South American name for hyperactive female
cats. Colombia is a South American country
famous for its coffee and its cocaine.

COLUMBUS   A good name for cats with an adventurous,
exploring streak. This is the name given to a
handsome stripy grey tom-cat I know who
once fell out of a fourth-floor window on his
explorations!

CONFUCIUS   A Chinese name for philosophical tom-cats.
Confucius was a famous Chinese philosopher

who founded the influential philosophy of Confucianism.

CONRAD A literary name for adventurous male cats, especially those living by the sea. Joseph Conrad, a novelist whose works include *The Heart of Darkness* and *Lord Jim*, spent much of his youth as a sailor and set many of his books in the sea-faring world.

CONSTANTINOPLE An exotic name for male cats. Constantinople was the former ancient name of what is now Istanbul, Turkey's capital.

COOKIE The perfect name for biscuit-coloured cats. 'Cookies' is the American word for biscuits.

COPPER A metal-inspired name especially suitable for Red Abyssinians. Copper, a reddish-brown metal, was named after the island of Cyprus, which was the metal's chief source during Roman times.

CORA A Greek name, suitable for female cats. It comes from the Greek *kore*, meaning 'maiden'.

CORAL A marine name for female cats. Corals are tiny marine animals who secrete a stiff, external skeleton and the name comes from the Greek *korallion*, meaning 'pebble'.

CORKY A humorous name for cats, derived from Corky the Cat of cartoon fame.

CORNELIUS An old-fashioned name for male cats. It comes from the Latin *corneus*, meaning 'hard-hearted'.

CORNWALL A traditional English name for independent male cats. Cornwall is England's most south-western county and has a strong sense of identity.

COUSCOUS A Moroccan name, suitable for cats of either sex. Couscous, made from dried semolina, is eaten as a staple in North Africa.

CRACKERS The affectionately appropriate name for a black-and-white cat who drove its owner mad!

CROMWELL A stern name for tough, dominating tom-cats. Cromwell was the English soldier and statesman who overthrew Charles I and subsequently became Lord Protector.

CRUMPET A homely name for domestic cats of either sex.

Crumpets are soft yeast cakes traditionally eaten at tea-time.

CRUSOE   For solitary tom-cats, a name inspired by castaway Robinson Crusoe. In Daniel Defoe's famous novel Robinson Crusoe is shipwrecked and has to cope with life on a desert island.

CRYSTAL   An elegant name for bright-eyed female cats. Crystal is a clear, ice-like mineral, known for its brightness and clarity. The name comes from Greek *krustallos*, meaning 'ice'.

CUBA   An exotic, tropical name for cats of either sex. Cuba is a Caribbean country off the south coast of Florida.

CUCUMBER   A cool, summery name for cats of either sex, inspired by the long, green juicy vegetable.

CUPID   A mythological name for much-loved male cats. In Roman mythology Cupid was the god of love, often portrayed as a small boy shooting arrows of love from his bow.

CUSTARD The sardonic, drawling cat who sparred with Roobarb the dog in the children's cartoon series *Roobarb and Custard*.

CUTHBERT An Old English name for male cats. The name comes from Old English *cuth*, meaning 'famous', and *beohrt*, meaning 'bright'.

CYRANO A poetic name for dashing tom-cats with long snouts. Cyrano de Bergerac, immortalized in Rostand's eponymous play, was a chivalrous writer famous for his comically long nose.

DAISY   A floral-inspired name for pretty female cats. The name comes from the Old English *goegeseage*, meaning 'day's eye', because of the flower's similarity to an open eye.

DALI   An artistic name for mad tom-cats. Salvador Dali was the famous Spanish surrealist who portrayed the subconscious with a photographic level of realism in his paintings.

DAMSON   A fruit-inspired name for cats of either sex. Damsons are purple-skinned plum-like fruit with a tart flavour.

DANDY   A dashing name for debonair male cats. Dandy is the term given to a man inordinately devoted to smart attire.

DANTE   A poetic name for thoughtful male cats. Dante

was the famous medieval Italian poet who wrote the epic poem *The Divine Comedy*.

DAPHNE A feminine name for tree-loving felines. In Greek mythology Daphne was a nymph who, while trying to escape from Apollo's advances, was transformed into a laurel tree.

DARJEELING An Indian name for domestic cats of either sex. Darjeeling, a town in West Bengal, is a major tea-growing centre.

D'ARTAGNAN A dashing French name for adventurous tom-cats. In Dumas' novel *The Three Musketeers*, D'Artagnan is the idealistic would-be musketeer from Gascony.

DATA A *Star Trek: The Next Generation*-inspired name for intelligent technocats.

DAUPHIN A French name for regal male cats. Until 1350 to 1830 Dauphin was the title of heirs to the French crown.

DEAN For rebellious, lean tom-cats. James Dean, who starred in *Rebel Without a Cause* and *East of Eden* before dying young, epitomized teenage rebellion and angst in the 1950s.

DEGAS   An artistic name for graceful male cats. French painter and sculptor Edgar Degas was noted for his portrayals of ballet and racecourses.

DELHI   An Indian name for cats of either sex. Delhi, situated between the Ganges and Indus valleys, is the capital of India.

DELIUS   A musical name for romantic male cats. Composer Frederick Delius is known for lyrical works such as *Appalachia* and *Paris, the Song of the Great City*.

DELPHI   A Greek name for perceptive female felines. In ancient Greece, Delphi was the site of the oracle of Apollo.

DEMETER   A mythological name for fruitful female felines. In Greek mythology, Demeter was the Greek corn goddess, mother of Persephone.

DERBY   For fleet-footed cats of either sex. The Derby is a famous flat race for three-year-old horses over 1.5 miles (2.4 km) at Epsom.

DERWENT A river-inspired name for male cats with a penchant for water. The Derwent is the name of several rivers in England.

DETROIT A rugged American name for tom-cats who enjoy car travel. A city in Michigan, USA, Detroit was traditionally dominated by the motor-vehicle industry.

DEUTERONOMY A venerable name, after T. S. Eliot's long-lived cat. In 'Old Deuteronomy', the ancient feline is described as 'a cat who has lived many lives in succession'.

DIABOLO For mischievous male cats with a bit of the devil in them. Diabolo, a game with a two-headed top caught on string, was originally called 'devil on two sticks'.

DIAGHILEV A Russian name for charismatic cats. Sergei Diaghilev was the influential Russian impresario who discovered Nijinsky.

DIAMOND A jewel-inspired name for cats with sparkling eyes. Diamond gemstones are prized for their sparkle.

DIANA A suitable name for predatory female felines with a penchant for nocturnal excursions. Diana was the Roman goddess of the hunt, associated with the moon.

DICKENS A literary name for energetic tom-cats. Victorian novelist Charles Dickens was noted for his prodigious output.

DIDO A regal name for passionate female felines. Dido was the legendary Queen of Carthage who in Virgil's *Aeneid* killed herself when abandoned by her lover Aeneas.

DIGBY A down-to-earth masculine name for curious tom-cats. The name comes from the Old French *diguer*, meaning to 'make a ditch' or 'to unearth'.

DIJON A French name for mustard-coloured cats. Dijon, the former capital of Burgundy in France, is famous for its mustard.

DILL A herb-inspired name for fish-loving cats of either sex. Feathery dill is valued especially by the Scandinavians, who use it with fish in dishes such as gravlax.

DINKY A toy-inspired name for small cats of either sex. Dinky toys make small-scale toys, famously cars.

DIRK A handsome name for intelligent male cats, inspired by the actor Dirk Bogarde. In his youth Bogarde was a matinée idol before he changed his image by working with European directors such as Visconti and Fassbinder.

DISRAELI For flamboyant male cats, inspired by the Victorian politician Benjamin Disraeli, conservative Prime Minister under Queen Victoria, who was noted for his wit and flair.

DIXIE An American name for musical cats of either sex. Dixieland jazz was played by white musicians imitating traditional New Orleans style.

DIZZY For rhythmic tom-cats, after Dizzy Gillespie. Gillespie was the black jazz trumpeter who was one of the originators of bebop.

DJANGO Again, for rhythmic tom-cats, after jazzman Django Reinhardt. The jazz guitarist of gipsy origin worked with Stephane Grappelli.

DOLLY A quintessentially feminine name, given to a huge, rather dim, grey tabby of my acquaintance who lapped up affection. Famous Dollys include American singer and actress Dolly Parton.

DOLORES A romantic Spanish name for female cats. Dolores comes from the Latin for 'lady of sorrows'.

DOMINGO An operatic name for plump, vocal tom-cats.

47

Opera singer Placido Domingo acquired superstar status when he sang for the World Cup in Italy.

DOMINICA   A Caribbean name for female felines. Dominica is an island in the West Indies, the largest of the Windward Islands.

DON JUAN   For seductive tom-cats, after the legendary lover Don Juan. This aristocratic libertine crops up repeatedly in European culture from Molière's play *Don Juan* to Mozart's opera *Don Giovanni*.

DONATELLO   An artistic name for graceful male cats. Donatello, the Renaissance Florentine sculptor, is famous for his life-like works such as the statue of David.

DORIS   A homely 1950s name for female cats, inspired by American movie actress Doris Day. In a series of domestic comedies Doris Day came to epitomize the wholesome 'girl next door'.

DRYDEN   A poetic name for male cats. The poet John Dryden was noted for his witty verse satires and plays such as *Marriage à la Mode*.

DUBLIN An Irish name for male cats. Dublin is the capital of Ireland, a city noted for its literary connections.

DUCHESS An aristocratic name, after the elegant white female feline star of Disney's *The Aristocats*.

DUFY An artistic name for male cats. The French painter Raoul Dufy is noted for his use of colour in lively scenes, such as regattas and horse-races.

DUKE For cool cats, after American jazzman Duke Ellington (1899–1974). A composer, band leader and pianist, Ellington was a leading light in the American jazz scene.

DUMAS A literary name for swashbuckling tom-cats, after the creator of *The Three Musketeers*. Alexandre Dumas was noted for his historical romances, including *The Count of Monte Cristo*.

DYLAN A laid-back name for vocal male cats. American singer and songwriter Bob Dylan was a key voice of the 1960s protest movement with albums such as *The Times They Are A-Changin'*.

EARL   An aristocratic name for noble tom-cats. The name comes from the Old English *eorl*, meaning 'nobleman' or 'chief'.

EARTHA   A seductive name, after feline chanteuse Eartha Kitt. With her distinctive husky voice she starred as a sexy Catwoman in a cult TV *Batman* series.

EBENEEZER   An old-fashioned name for male cats. Famous Ebeneezers include Ebeneezer Scrooge in Dickens's heart-warming tale *A Christmas Carol*.

EBONY   An elegant name for attractive black cats of either sex. Ebony is the dark heartwood from tropical trees, used in inlaying and cabinetwork.

ECUADOR   A South American name for male cats. Ecuador is a South American country named after the Equator, on which it lies.

EDDIE   A comic name for male cats. Eddie Izzard is a highly individual stand-up comic with a penchant for cats.

EGYPT   An exotic name for Sphinx-like cats of either sex. Egypt houses the historic remains of its great past, including the Sphinx and the pyramids.

EIFFEL   A masculine French name for high-climbing cats. Engineer Alexandre-Gustave Eiffel built the 984ft (300m) metal Eiffel Tower in 1889 and it remained the world's tallest building until 1930.

EINSTEIN   A masculine name for brainy beasts. Albert Einstein was the Nobel Prize-winning German physicist who discovered the theory of relativity.

EISENSTEIN   A Russian name for ingenious male cats. Sergei Eisenstein was the Russian film director whose films *Battleship Potemkin* and *Ivan the Terrible* used innovative editing and montage techniques.

ELBA   For solitary cats of either sex. Elba was the Italian island of Napoleon's exile between 1814 and 1815.

ELDORADO   An exotic name for treasured male cats. From the Spanish for 'the golden one', Eldorado was the fabled region of great wealth which the Spanish conquistadors sought for in South America.

ELECTRA   A legendary name for strong-willed female felines. In Greek legend Electra helped her brother Orestes escape after Agamemnon's murder.

ELGAR   A distinguished name for musical male cats. The British composer Edward Elgar was noted for works including *The Enigma Variations* and *Pomp and Circumstance*.

ELIOT   A male name in tribute to poet T. S. Eliot, creator of *Old Possum's Book of Practical Cats*.

ELIZABETH   A regal female cat name. Famous Elizabeths include the charismatic Queen Elizabeth I. Elizabeth II is a contemporary royal example.

ELLA   The name of a diminutive black cat of my acquaintance, christened after black American chanteuse Ella Fitzgerald, who performed with musicians such as Duke Ellington and Oscar Peterson.

ELLINGTON   For rhythmic tom-cats, after American jazz pianist, composer and band leader Duke Ellington.

ELTON   A pop-inspired name for energetic tom-cats. The British rock pianist and singer Elton John became popular with hits like *Rocket Man*.

ELVIS   For rock 'n' roll cats with rhythmic hips. American singer Elvis Presley revolutionized pop music during the 1950s with songs like *Hound Dog* and *Don't Be Cruel*.

EMERALD   A jewel-inspired name for green-eyed cats of either sex. A green variety of beryl, emeralds are valued as gemstones.

EMMA   A dainty literary name for strong-willed female felines. Emma is the heroine of Jane Austen's witty eponymous novel.

ENDIVE   A vegetable-inspired name for cats of either sex. Endive, also known as chicory, is a salad vegetable with a distinctive, slightly bitter flavour.

ENDYMION   A legendary name for handsome male cats who

enjoy napping. In Greek mythology Endymion was the beautiful youth who was put to an enchanted, eternal sleep by Selene, goddess of the moon, so she could enjoy his beauty forever.

EPICURUS   For male cats with a penchant for good living. The Greek philosopher Epicurus founded Epicureanism in 300 BC in Athens, a philosophy which teaches that pleasure is the highest good.

EROS   A mythological name for lovable male cats. In Greek mythology Eros was the god of love, often portrayed armed with a bow and arrow.

ERROL   A Hollywood-inspired name for dashing, handsome tom-cats. Hollywood actor Errol Flynn starred as the adventurous hero in films such as *Captain Blood* and *The Adventures of Robin Hood*.

ETON   An upper-class name for male cats. Eton College is the famous public school founded by Henry VI in 1440.

EUCALYPTUS   For tree-climbing cats of either sex. Eucalyptus trees are native to Australia and contain essential oils.

EUGÈNIE A French name for regal female felines, after Napoleon III's consort. The name comes from the Greek for 'well-born'.

EVE A quintessentially female name, from the Hebrew *hawwah*, meaning 'breath of life'. This was the name of the first woman, according to Christianity.

EVEREST For adventurous, high-climbing tom-cats. Mount Everest is the highest mountain in the world, dominating the Himalayas.

EXCALIBUR A mythic name for sharp-clawed tom-cats. Exacalibur was King Arthur's magical sword which upon his death was thrown back to the Lady of the Lake.

FABERGÉ   A Russian name for precious cats of either sex. Peter Carl Fabergé was the Russian jeweller and goldsmith, famed for the intricate jewelled Easter eggs that he created for the Tsar and his family.

FAYE   For coolly beautiful female felines, inspired by actress Faye Dunaway. The name comes from the Old French *fei*, meaning 'fairy'.

FELICE   An Italian name for good-natured cats of either sex. *Felice* is Italian for 'happy'.

FELIX   An appropriate name for cheeky black cats, inspired by the ink-black cartoon cat. Felix is an especially appropriate name for cats as the naturalists' term for domesticated cats is *felis domestica*.

FELLINI   A cinema-inspired Italian name for tom-cats.

Federico Fellini was the innovative director such films as *La Dolce Vita* and *8½*.

FENNEL   A spice-inspired name for cats of either sex. Fennel seeds are used to flavour both sweet and savoury dishes.

FERDINAND   An appropriate name for belligerent tom-cats. Ferdinand comes from the Latin for 'war-like'.

FIAT   A car-inspired name for tom-cats. Fiat is the popular Italian car manufacturer, makers of cars including the tiny Cinquecento.

FIFI   A dainty name with a French flavour for female felines.

FIJI   A tropical name for cats of either sex. The Fiji Islands in the Pacific are depicted as a tropical paradise.

FLAMENCO   A Spanish name for graceful cats of either sex. Flamenco is the famous Spanish dance, at once elegant and passionate.

FLAUBERT   A French name for male cats. Gustave Flaubert

was the nineteenth-century French novelist, author of *Madame Bovary*.

FLITTER An appropriate name for alert, nervy cats of either sex. To flit is to move lightly and softly.

FLORA A mythological name for flower-loving female cats. Flora, from the Latin *floris* for 'flower', was the Roman goddess of blossoming plants.

FLORENCE An old-fashioned feminine name, often abbreviated to Flo. Famous examples include nurse Florence Nightingale and the unflappable Florence from the children's TV series *The Magic Roundabout*.

FLORIDA An American name for sun-loving female cats. Florida is a sub-tropical south-eastern American state famous for its beach resorts such as Palm Beach and Miami Beach.

FLUFF An appropriate name for long-haired cats of either sex.

FLYNN A Gaelic name for ginger tom-cats. In Gaelic it means 'Son of the red-haired man'.

FONTEYN   A ballet-inspired name for graceful female cats. Margot Fonteyn was the famous ballerina whose dancing partnership with Nureyev was legendary.

FOXY   For attractive ginger cats of either sex. Foxy conveys both the colour of the cat and also means 'attractive'.

FRANCHETTE   A French name for beautiful female felines. It is the elegant name given to Claudine's beloved cat in Colette's novel *Claudine at School*.

FRANCIS   A male name for independent tom-cats. Francis comes from the Latin *franciscus*, meaning 'a free man'. Famous examples include the animal-loving St Francis of Assisi.

FRANGIPANI   An exotic name for beautiful female felines. Frangipani are sweet-scented tropical flowers, prized for their fragrance.

FRANKINCENSE   A biblical name for cats of either sex. Frankincense was one of the gifts brought by the Three Kings to the baby Jesus and is an aromatic gum used in incense.

FRED   A Hollywood-inspired name for agile and graceful tom-cats. Tap-dancer Fred Astaire, star of films such as *Top Hat* and *Silk Stockings*, was famous for his elegant dancing and nimble footwork.

FREUD   For thoughtful male cats. The Austrian psychiatrist Sigmund Freud was a pioneer of psychoanalysis.

FRISCO   A Californian name for laid-back male cats.
            'Frisco' is the abbreviation of San Francisco, the
            famous Californian city.

FRISKY   An appropriate name for energetic, playful cats of
            either sex. To frisk is to leap about playfully.

FROOTBAT   The affectionate name given by a friend of mine
            to a mad, fluffy, pretty grey tabby with a very
            sweet nature.

FUCHSIA   A floral name for beautiful female cats. Fuchsia is
            a type of flowering shrub with distinctive scarlet
            flowers.

FUDGE   A confectionery-inspired name for sweet-natured,
            caramel-coloured felines of either sex. Fudge is a
            toffee-like sweet made from sugar, butter and
            milk.

FUJI   A Japanese name for high-climbing cats of either
            sex. Mount Fuji is the highest mountain in Japan,
            regarded as a symbol of the country.

FURRY   An appropriate name for cats of either sex.

GABRIEL   A name for angelic male cats. The archangel Gabriel told the Virgin Mary that she was going to be the mother of Jesus.

GALAHAD   An Arthurian name for noble male cats. In the legends of King Arthur, Galahad was a shining example of knighthood, succeeding in the quest for the Holy Grail.

GALÁPAGOS   An exotic name for huge, slow-moving male cats. The Galápagos islands off Ecuador are famous for their giant tortoises, which grow up to 1.5m (4ft) long.

GALILEO   An Italian name for inventive male cats. The mathematician, physicist and astronomer Galileo is credited with many discoveries, among them that the rate of fall of a body is independent of its mass.

GALINGALE An exotic spice-inspired name for cats of either
sex. Galingale is an aromatic rhizome used in
South East Asian cookery.

GARBO An elegant name for reclusive, beautiful female
felines. Greta Garbo, the star of films such as
Camille, was noted for her aloof beauty and her
reclusiveness.

GARCÍA A Latin American name for male cats. Gabriel
García Marquez is the famous Colombian writer,
author of *One Hundred Years of Solitude*.

GARIBALDI An Italian name for independent-minded male
cats. Giuseppe Garibaldi was an Italian soldier
who fought for the unification of Italy.

GARLIC A culinary name for cats of either sex. Garlic is a
pungent bulb used to flavour dishes and also
attributed with aphrodisiac properties.

GARRICK The perfect name for thespian cats. David Garrick
was a notable eighteenth-century actor-manager
after whom the Garrick Club in London is named.

GARRISON An American name for laid-back tom-cats.

Author Garrison Keillor has won over both American and British audiences with his Mid-West tales of small-town life set in the imaginary town of Lake Wobegon.

GASCONY   A French name for male cats. Gascony was a former duchy of south-west France, which still retains a strong regional sense of identity.

GATTO   An Italian name for cats of either sex. *Gatto* is Italian for 'cat'.

GAZZA   A football name for agile tom-cats, inspired by the popular British footballer.

GEMINI   An elegant astrological name for cats born between 21 May and 21 June. Gemini is the sign of the Heavenly Twins and people under its sign are characterized by their dual nature.

GENGHIS KHAN   A warlike name for ferocious male cats. Genghis Khan was the Mongol warlord who founded the Mongol Empire in Central Asia.

GEOFF   The name of a handsome tabby I know of, named after Sheffield Theatre manager Geoffrey Ost.

GEORGE A traditional English name for male cats. St George is the patron saint of England, noted for his battle with a dragon.

GERALD A masculine name for tom-cats, inspired by animal-lover and author Gerald Durrell.

GERANIUM A flower-inspired name for cats of either sex. Geraniums are popular flowering garden plants, noted for their vigour and hardiness.

GERSHWIN A music-inspired name for elegant tom-cats. US composer and songwriter George Gershwin is famous for his many melodious songs as well as the opera *Porgy and Bess*.

GIACOMETTI An artistic name for slender tom-cats. Sculptor Alberto Giacometti is famous for his distinctive stick-like forms.

GILLESPIE For cool tom-cats, inspired by jazz musician Dizzy Gillespie, the American jazz trumpeter and originator of bebop.

GINA A name for garden-loving female cats. The name comes from the Hebrew for 'garden'.

GINGER   A classic name for ginger-coloured toms. It was used by Beatrix Potter for the 'yellow tom-cat' in *The Tale of Ginger and Pickles*.

GINKGO   A plant-inspired name for oriental cats of either sex. Ginkgo, also called maidenfair tree, is native to China and grown both for ornament and for its edible nuts.

GINSENG   An oriental name for cats of either sex. Ginseng is a Eastern root used in oriental medicine and valued for its aphrodisiac qualities.

GLOUCESTER   An English name for male cats. Gloucester is a market town in west England noted for its cathedral.

GOA   An exotic name for beautiful female felines. Goa is the Indian state famed for its palm-fringed beaches.

GOLDIE   For feminine golden-furred felines, inspired by actress Goldie Hawn with her 'dizzy blonde' screen persona.

GOLDWYN   For dominating male cats. Hollywood mogul Sam Goldwyn was noted for his fiery temper.

GOLIATH   A biblical name for giant tom-cats. Goliath was the Philistine giant whom David took on and slew.

GOTH   A historical name for ferocious tom-cats. The Goths were the Germanic people who invaded the Roman Empire.

GRACE   An elegant name for graceful female felines. Grace comes from the Latin *gratus*, meaning 'pleasing'.

GRANTA   A literary name for cats of either sex. *Granta* is the literary 'magazine' with notable contemporary writers as contributors.

GRAPPELLI   For lively tom-cats. French jazz violinist Stephane Grappelli has recorded with Yehudi Menuhin.

GREENGAGE   A fruit-inspired name for sweet-natured cats of either sex. Greengage, a member of the plum family, is a honey-sweet fruit.

GREENWICH   A nautical name for adventurous male cats. Greenwich, a London borough on the River Thames, is the home of the tea clipper *Cutty Sark* and Sir Francis Chichester's *Gipsy Moth IV*.

GRENADA   A tropical name for female cats. Grenada is an island in the West Indies famous for its nutmeg.

GRIDDLEBONE   From T. S. Eliot's *Old Possum's Book of Practical Cats*. Griddlebone is Growltiger's faithless female companion.

GRIFFIN   A mythological name for leonine cats of either sex. The griffin is a mythological creature with a lion's body and the head and wings of an eagle.

GRIMALKIN   A traditional cat's name, especially used for black cats. The name has ancient associations with witchcraft and magic.

GROUCHO   For humorous or grouchy tom-cats. Comedian Groucho Marx, star of films like *A Night at the Opera* and *Duck Soup*, was noted for his abrasive, wisecracking humour.

GROWLTIGER   T. S. Eliot's rough 'Bravo cat' from *Old Possum's Book of Practical Cats*. In the poem 'Growltiger's Last Stand' Growltiger is surrounded by Siamese and 'forced to walk the plank'.

GUAVA   A fruit-inspired name for female cats. The guava is a sweet-fleshed, fig-shaped tropical fruit.

GUCCI   A designer name for chic male cats. Gucci shoes and luggage, made by the Italian company, have distinct 'snob' value.

GUINEVERE   A regal name for queenly female white cats. In Arthurian legend Guinevere, from the Welsh *gwyn*, meaning 'white', was the name of King Arthur's beautiful wife.

GUINNESS   An Irish-inspired name for dark brown and cream tom-cats. Guinness is a famous dark brown Irish stout, noted for its strength.

GULLIVER   A literary name for adventurous male cats. Gulliver is the hero of Jonathan Swift's satirical novel *Gulliver's Travels*.

GUMBO   A food-inspired name for plump tom-cats. Gumbo is a famous Creole soup-cum-stew, often made using okra and seafood.

GUS   The name of T. S. Eliot's 'theatre cat'. In *Old Possum's Book of Practical Cats*, Gus appears as 'the cat at the theatre door', reminiscing about his days of glory 'as Firefrorefiddle, the Fiend of the Fell'.

HADDOCK A piscine name for irascible, fish-loving tom-cats. The haddock is a popular sea fish. Captain Haddock is the name of the irritable nautical sea-dog in Hergé's Tintin books.

HADRIAN A Roman name for imperial male cats with a penchant for climbing walls. Hadrian was the Roman Emperor who ordered the building of Hadrian's Wall in Britain, designed to contain the Scottish tribes.

HAGGIS A Scottish name for plump male cats. The haggis is a traditional Scottish meat dish made from sheep's innards and oatmeal stuffed into a bag made from the sheep's stomach.

HALIFAX A Yorkshire name for sturdy tom-cats. Halifax is a Yorkshire town with a strong woollen textile tradition.

HAMMETT A literary name for tough, intelligent tom-cats. The American writer Dashiell Hammett worked as a private eye before writing his famous gritty detective stories.

HAMPSTEAD An elegant, London-inspired name for male cats. Hampstead is an area of north London noted for its literary and artistic connections.

HANCOCK For morose or comic tom-cats. Comedian Tony Hancock, famous for his 1950s radio series *Hancock's Half Hour*, had a distinctive melancholy humour.

HANNIBAL A distinguished name for fighting tom-cats. Hannibal was a Carthaginian general, famed for his crossing of the Alps in winter. Also an appropriate name for murderous tom-cats, after Hannibal Lecter, the serial killer in Thomas Harris's best-selling thriller *The Silence of the Lambs*.

HARLEQUIN For mischievous, acrobatic male cats. Harlequin is a comic lover figure in *commedia dell'arte*.

HARLEY A good name for speedy macho tom-cats, inspired by the famous Harley Davidson motorbikes.

HARRY   A traditional name for male cats. Harry is a version of Henry, a name with royal connotations in Britain.

HAVANA   An exotic name for female cats. Havana is the capital of Cuba, the Caribbean island.

HAWAII   A tropical name for graceful female cats. Hawaii is a chain of Pacific islands known for its palm-lined beaches.

HAZEL   For brown-eyed female cats. Hazel is the name of an edible nut and also of a reddish-brown colour. It was a popular female name in the nineteenth century.

HAZLITT   A literary name for male cats. William Hazlitt (1778–1830) was a witty and incisive British essayist and literary critic, author of *The Spirit of the Age*.

HECTOR   A heroic name from Greek mythology for fierce tom-cats. Hector, son of Priam, King of Troy, killed Patroclus and was in turn killed by Achilles.

HECUBA   A legendary name for queenly female cats.

Hecuba was the wife of Priam, King of Troy, and mother of the Trojan warrior Hector.

HEINZ   A name for moggies of mixed origins. Heinz, the famous manufacturers of baked beans, is known for making '57 varieties'.

HELEN   A suitable name for beautiful female felines. In Greek legend the beautiful Helen, wife of Menelaus, fled to Troy with Paris, thus triggering the Trojan War.

HELSINKI   A Finnish name for city cats of either sex. Helsinki is the capital of Finland.

HEMINGWAY   A rugged male name for tough tom-cats. The American writer Ernest Hemingway, author of *The Old Man and the Sea*, was a great lover of cats.

HENNA   For ginger cats of either sex. The leaves of the henna shrub are used to dye hair red.

HENRIETTA   An elegant name, suitable for dainty, regal female cats. Henrietta Maria was the wife of Charles I.

HENRY   A traditional name for regal male cats. Henry has

been the name of eight kings of England. The name comes from Old German, meaning 'house' and 'power'.

HERCULES A mythological name suitable for strong, heroic tom-cats. In Greek mythology the hero Hercules performed huge feats of courage and strength.

HERMES A legendary name for swift male cats. In Greek mythology Hermes was the messenger of the gods, often portrayed wearing winged sandals.

HERO A noble name suitable for cats of either sex. Hero is both a female name and the word to describe a man of superhuman qualities.

HIAWATHA For heroic tom-cats, after the legendary Native American chief. Hiawatha, chief of the Onondaga tribe, was immortalized in Longfellow's poem *Song of Hiawatha*.

HICKORY A tree-inspired name for smoke-coloured tom-cats. The hickory tree is native to North America and hickory chips were used to flavour smoked meats.

HIGHGATE A London-inspired name for city-loving male cats. There is a statue of Dick Whittington's faithful cat on Highgate Hill.

HILLARY For tom-cats who enjoy climbing and exploring. In 1953 mountaineer Sir Edmund Hillary, with Tenzing Norgay, were the first human beings to reach the summit of Mount Everest.

HILTON A hotel-inspired name for elegant male cats. The Hilton hotels are famous around the world.

HINCA The name of Scottish author Sir Walter Scott's 'favourite cat' and 'old friend', who valiantly and fearlessly taunted large dogs until killed by the young bloodhound Nimrod.

HOCKNEY An artistic name for male cats. British painter David Hockney is famous for his colourful and witty paintings.

HODGE The name of Dr Johnson's cat for whom, according to Boswell's *Life of Samuel Johnson*, 'he himself used to go out and buy oysters'. Boswell also records Johnson, having admitted to liking other cats better than Hodge, 'as if perceiving Hodge to be out of countenance, adding, "But he is a very fine cat, a very fine cat indeed." '

HOLIDAY   For vocal female felines. American black jazz singer Billie Holiday, also known as 'Lady Day', sang with Count Basie and Artie Shaw.

HOLLY   The perfect name for sharp-clawed Christmas kittens. Holly, the prickly-leafed evergreen shrub, is traditionally a Christmas decoration.

HOLLYWOOD   A cinema-inspired name for glamorous cats of either sex. Hollywood, a suburb of Los Angeles in California, is the focus of the US film industry.

HOMER   A poetic name for wise tom-cats. Homer was the blind Greek epic poet, author of the *Iliad* and the *Odyssey*.

HONEY   An endearing name for sweet-natured female cats. Honey, a thick syrup produced by bees, is a natural sweetener.

HONG KONG   An oriental name for food-loving cats. Hong Kong, the prosperous island off the south coast of China, is famous for its excellent Chinese food.

HORACE A poetic Roman name suitable for tom-cats. Horace was a leading poet under the Emperor Augustus, famous for his *Odes* and *Epistles* portraying contemporary Roman society.

HOUDINI For adventurous cats with a penchant for escaping. Harry Houdini, the intrepid escapologist and musician, was known for his ability to escape from locked containers, even under water.

HUGO A dignified name for male cats. The name comes from the Celtic *hu*, meaning 'inspiration', or from the Old German name Huguberht, meaning 'intelligent and noble'.

HUMPHREY A political name for suave tom-cats. Humphrey is the Downing Street tom-cat, presumably named after Sir Humphrey of the *Yes Minister* TV series, and defended against accusations of duckling-stealing by Prime Minister John Major.

HYACINTH A flower-inspired name for female cats. Hyacinth flowers, grown from bulbs, have a distinctive sweet perfume.

INCA   An ancient name for female cats. The Incas were an Indian people of Peru who established an empire from Ecuador to Chile during the fifteenth century.

INDIA   An exotic name for beautiful female felines, especially appropriate for oriental cats. The subcontinent of India borders Pakistan, China, Nepal, Bhutan and Burma.

IRIS   A mythological name for beautiful female cats. In Greek mythology Iris was the goddess of the rainbow and messenger of the gods.

ISADORA   A name for graceful female cats. The American dancer Isadora Duncan was famous for her innovative modern dancing.

IVAN A Russian name for imperial tom-cats. Ivan the Great, Grand Prince of Moscow, expanded Russian territory, while Ivan the Terrible was crowned Tsar in 1547.

IVOR A music-inspired name for graceful tom-cats. The British actor and composer Ivor Novello was famous for a series of romantic musicals, including *The Dancing Years*.

IVY An old-fashioned feminine name for cats of a clinging nature. The climbing plant ivy was a symbol of fidelity.

JACK   An English name for ingenious male cats. In the old English fairy-tale *Jack and the Beanstalk*, Jack outwits a ferocious giant, escaping with the giant's treasure.

JACQUELINE   An elegant French name for female felines. Famous Jacquelines include Jacqueline Kennedy, later Jacqueline Onassis, noted for her elegance and grace.

JADE   An oriental name for green-eyed female felines. Jade, a green semiprecious stone, has been valued since ancient times and is a symbol of longevity in China.

JAFFA   A biscuit-inspired name for marmalade-coloured cats of either sex. Jaffa Cakes are chocolate-coated biscuits with a marmalade filling.

JAMAICA   A tropical name for cats of either sex. Jamaica is
          an island country in the Caribbean, famous for its
          Blue Mountain coffee.

JASMINE   A flower-inspired name particularly suitable for
          dainty female white cats. White-flowering jasmine
          is noted for its fragrant scent and its essential oil is
          used in perfumery.

JASON   The name of the elegant Siamese in the children's
          TV programme *Blue Peter*, often calmly seated on
          Valerie Singleton's knee. In Greek mythology
          Jason was the name of a hero who, with the
          Argonauts, underwent many adventures on a
          quest to fetch the Golden Fleece.

JASPER   A stone-inspired name for bright-eyed tom-cats.
          Jasper is a semiprecious variety of chalcedony,
          often red or reddish-brown.

JAVA   An exotic name for cats of either sex, particularly
          coffee-coloured ones. Java, an island in the
          Indonesian archipelago, is noted for its rich
          coffee.

JAWS   The perfect name for a killer cat! *Jaws* is the title of Steven Spielberg's 1975 hit film about a killer shark that terrorizes a seaside community.

JAZZ   A music-inspired name for cats of either sex. Jazz, which originated with the black American community, is characterized by improvisation, strong rhythm and syncopation.

JEAN   An elegant female name, derived from the French Jeanne. Famous Jeans include cool American blonde actress Jean Arthur.

JEHOVAH   The name given to a vocal, sharp-faced Siamese inspired by a chance visit from a Jehovah's Witness on the day the kitten arrived in the house.

JELLICLE   For fun-loving, small, black-and-white cats of either sex, after the T. S. Eliot poem. In *The Song of the Jellicles* he describes them having 'cheerful faces' and 'bright black eyes'.

JELLY   A food-inspired name for sweet-natured cats of either sex. Jelly is a popular dessert and classic of children's parties.

JEMIMA   An old-fashioned feminine name for docile cats.
          The name comes from the Arabic *jomina*, meaning
          'dove'.

JENNIE   A feminine cat's name, given to the feline heroine
          of Paul Gallico's eponymous novel about a boy
          turned into a cat who is lovingly protected by
          Jennie.

JENNYANYDOTS   T. S. Eliot's domestic-natured 'gumbie cat', from
          'The Old Gumbie Cat', with 'tiger stripes and
          leopard spots' who 'sits and sits and sits and sits'.

JEOFFREY The name given to the eighteenth-century poet
          Christopher Smart's cat, immortalized in Smart's
          wonderful piece of poetry *My Cat Jeoffrey from
          Jubilate Agno*. An especially appropriate name for
          striped cats, as Jeoffrey 'is of the tribe of Tiger'.

JEREMY   A biblical name for male cats. Famous Jeremys
          include philosopher Jeremy Bentham, who pro-
          pounded utilitarianism.

JEROME   A biblical name for saintly male cats. St Jerome
          translated the Bible from Hebrew into Latin.

JESSIE A Scottish name for female cats, a version of Janet.

JETHRO A biblical name for male cats. The name comes from the Hebrew for 'wealth' and 'abundance'.

JEZEBEL A biblical name for tempestuous female felines, inspired by the eponymous melodramatic 1937 Bette Davis film in which she plays the scheming protagonist.

JIMMY A name for cool tom-cats, inspired by 1950s heart-throb Jimmy Dean. In his films *East of Eden* and *Rebel Without A Cause*, Jimmy Dean epitomized the moody adolescent rebel.

JOAN For courageous female cats, after Joan of Arc, also known as the Maid of Orleans. She was the fifteenth-century French patriot who, inspired by heavenly voices, led the French troops to victory against the English before being captured and burnt at the stake.

JONSON A dramatic name for courtly cats. Playwright Ben Jonson was the author of *Volpone* and *The Alchemist* as well as several court masques.

JOSEPH   A biblical name for grey tom-cats. Joseph Frere, adviser to Cardinal Richelieu, was known as the *éminence grise* because he wore grey robes.

JOSEPHINE   A dainty name for imperial female cats. The Empress Josephine was Napoleon's first wife, noted for her ability in state affairs.

JOSH A male name, abbreviated from Joshua, which comes from the Hebrew *Yehoshua*, meaning 'God is my salvation.'

JUMBO A suitable name for large grey tom-cats. The name comes from the African *jumba*, meaning 'elephant', and is a classic name for elephants.

JUNE A feminine name, especially suitable for cats born in the month of June.

JUNIPER A shrub-inspired name for cats of either sex. Fragrant juniper berries are an essential ingredient of gin.

JUNO A Roman name for queenly female cats. In Roman mythology Juno was the wife of Jupiter, the principal Roman god.

JUPITER A Roman name for kingly tom-cats. In Roman mythology Jupiter was the leader of the gods. Jupiter is also the name of the largest planet in our solar system.

KABUKI   A Japanese name for dramatic cats. Kabuki is a form of Japanese popular theatre descended from the aristocratic No theatre during the seventeenth century.

KAFKA   A literary name for nervy male cats. Czech writer Franz Kafka was the author of *Metamorphosis* and *The Trial*, in which the individual is isolated in a hostile world.

KANSAS   An American name for male cats. Kansas is a Mid-Western state, America's primary wheat-growing area.

KAPOK   For silky-coated cats of either sex. The kapok or silk-cotton tree, native to tropical America, is cultivated for the fine hairs which cover the seeds and are used for stuffing mattresses.

KARATE   An oriental name for combative cats of either sex. Karate is a form of unarmed combat which originated in Japan and draws on ju-jitsu and Zen Buddhism.

KARLOFF   A film-inspired name for monstrously large male cats. Actor Boris Karloff became a star with the 1931 film of *Frankenstein*, after which he was often cast in sinister roles.

KEAN   A thespian name for theatrical male cats. British actor Edmund Kean was renowned for his passionate performances in *Othello*, *The Merchant of Venice* and *The Jew of Malta*.

KEATS   A poetic name for romantic male cats. British poet John Keats was a leading poet of the Romantic movement and the author of *Ode to a Nightingale*.

KEBAB   A food-inspired name for greedy tom-cats. The kebab is a popular take-away food.

KELLY   A Hollywood name for beautiful, elegant female cats. Cool blonde actress Grace Kelly was the aloof star of Hitchcock films *Rear Window* and *To Catch a Thief*.

KENDO   A Hollywood name for combative male cats. Kendo is a Japanese martial art using bamboo staffs and derived from samurai sword fighting.

KENYA   An African name for leonine cats of either sex. Kenya, the East African state, is famous for its wildlife reserves, home to lions, elephants and giraffes.

KENZO   A designer-inspired name for oriental male cats. Japanese fashion designer Kenzo is noted for his stylish clothes.

KETCHUP   A food-inspired name for cats of either sex. Tomato ketchup is a sauce made from tomatoes and used as a condiment.

KIKU   A Japanese name for female oriental cats. The name comes from the Japanese for 'chrysanthemum'.

KILLER   A classic name for predatory hunter cats.

KING   For regal male cats.

KIRK   A *Star Trek*-inspired name for vain tom-cats.

Captain James Kirk was commander of the Starship *Enterprise* in the popular TV series set in outer space.

KIT-KAT A chocolate-inspired name for brown cats of either sex. Kit-Kats are popular chocolate-covered wafer bars.

KITTY A classic kitten and cat name with feminine associations. Kitty is a popular name for kittens and also a variant of the female name Katherine.

KIWI An exotic fruit-inspired name, suitable for oriental cats of either sex. The kiwi fruit, also known as 'Chinese gooseberry', originated in China but was cultivated commercially in New Zealand.

KOH-I-NOOR A jewel-inspired name for bright-eyed cats. The Koh-i-Noor is a famous 108-carat diamond, originally owned by the Mogul dynasty but now in Queen Elizabeth II's coronation crown.

KUMQUAT A fruit-inspired name for cats of either sex. Kumquats are small Asian citrus fruit with a distinctive tangy flavour.

LADRO   From the Italian for 'thief'. This was the name my father gave to a roguish black cat who stole a leg of lamb from the kitchen before becoming a beloved family pet.

LANCASTER   A British name for independent-minded male cats. The Lancaster dynasty fought against the Yorkists in the Wars of the Roses.

LANCELOT   An Arthurian name for handsome male cats. Sir Lancelot was a heroic knight, leading light of the Round Table, who tragically fell in love with King Arthur's wife Guinevere.

LAUREN   A Hollywood name for beautiful green-eyed female felines. Husky-voiced actress Lauren Bacall starred with Humphrey Bogart in *To Have and To Have Not* and *The Big Sleep*.

LAVENDER A flower-inspired name for sweet-smelling cats of either sex. Lavender, with its fragrant leaves and flowers, has been a popular source of scent since the Middle Ages.

LEICA A camera-inspired name for sharp-eyed cats of either sex. The Leica is a prestigious camera, noted for its lens quality and famously used by photographer Henri Cartier-Bresson.

LEMON A fruit-inspired name for yellow-eyed cats of either sex. The yellow citrus fruit is a kitchen staple, used to flavour sweet and savoury dishes.

LENNOX The name given to a handsome black tom-cat I know, in tribute to boxer Lennox Lewis.

LENTIL A food-inspired name for cats of either sex. Lentil seeds are a protein-rich food.

LEO A distinguished name, particularly suitable for tawny tom-cats. The name evokes the cat's leonine ancestry and was also the Russian writer Tolstoy's first name. It is also apt for cats born between 23 July and 22 August, under the sign of Leo.

LEONARDO An Italian name for inventive male cats, inspired by the Renaissance genius Leonardo da Vinci whose talents included painting, engineering and architecture.

LEONE For tough, cool tom-cats, after the Spaghetti Western director Sergio Leone. An especially appropriate name for tawny tom-cats as *leone* is Italian for 'lion'.

LEOPARD For spotted cats of either sex. The leopard is a solitary and nocturnal large spotted cat found in Africa and Asia.

LETTUCE A salad-inspired name for garden-loving female cats. It comes from the Latin *laetitia*, meaning 'unrestrained joy'.

LEWIS A distinguished English name for magnificent male cats. Oxford don C. S. Lewis was the author of the popular Narnia series of children's books featuring Aslan the lion.

LIBRA A zodiac-inspired name for well-balanced cats born between 23 September and 22 October.

LILAC   A flower-inspired name for grey-furred female felines, especially apt for Russian Blues. Lilac is the name given to the warm-toned grey colour fur which some cats have.

LILLIE   For captivating female cats with a theatrical streak. Actress Lillie Langtry was noted for her beauty and was intimate with Edward VII while he was Prince of Wales.

LIMA   A South American name for female cats. Lima is the capital of Peru.

LIME   A tropical name for green-eyed cats of either sex. Green-skinned limes are tropical citrus fruits with a distinctive tangy flavour.

LINCOLN   A presidential name for dignified male cats. President Abraham Lincoln saw America through the Civil War and was assassinated in 1865 a few days after the South surrendered.

LINFORD   An athletic name for speedy tom-cats. Runner Linford Christie won the Olympic gold medal for the 100m race in the 1992 Barcelona Olympics.

LION A leonine name for regal, tawny tom-cats. The lion, known as 'the king of the beasts', is also associated with human majesty.

LIQUORICE For black cats of either sex. Liquorice root, with its black colour and flavour, is used in sweets.

LISBON A city-inspired name for male cats. Lisbon is the capital of Portugal.

LIZA A musical name for large-eyed vocal female felines. Singer and actress Liza Minnelli starred in the films *Cabaret* and *New York, New York* and continues a successful cabaret career.

LOGANBERRY A fruit-inspired name for soft-hearted cats of either sex. The soft fruit loganberry is a cross between the raspberry and the blackberry.

LOLITA A Nabokov-inspired name for nymphet kittens. Lolita was the eponymous heroine of Nabokov's controversial novel about a young girl obsessively desired by an older man.

LONDON A capital British name for city-dwelling tom-cats. London is the capital of Britain.

LOTUS   A flower-inspired name for serene female cats, especially appropriate for oriental cats. The lotus was a sacred flower in Ancient Egypt and is a symbol of Buddhism.

LOUIS   A French name for regal male cats. French monarch Louis XIV, also known as 'The Sun King', was a firm advocate of the divine right of kings.

LOUISE   A cinema-inspired name for sleek, elegant female felines. Beautiful actress Louise Brooks was a notable 1920s film star, most famously in *Pandora's Box*.

LUCIFER   A biblical name for proud, handsome tom-cats. Lucifer was the leader of the archangels until he rebelled against God and was cast into Hell where he became Satan.

LUCILLE   A TV name for whacky ginger-haired female felines. Red-headed comedienne Lucille Ball enjoyed TV stardom in America with the series *I Love Lucy*.

LUCKY An appropriate name for lucky black cats of either sex.

LUIS A Spanish name for inventive male cats. Luis Buñuel was a surrealist Spanish film director, noted for films such as *That Obscure Object of Desire*.

LUNA An Italian name suitable for night-loving cats of either sex. *Luna* is Italian for 'moon'.

LYCHEE An exotic name, suitable for oriental cats such as Burmese and Siamese. The lychee is a Chinese fruit with a distinctive sweet flavour.

LYNX For short-tailed cats with spotted fur. The lynx is a large cat with tufted ears, faintly spotted thick yellow fur and a short tail.

MAC — A short Scottish name for male cats. Mac is a classic Scottish prefix for names, e.g. MacDonald or Mackenzie.

MACAVITY — A name for stealthy ginger cats inspired by T. S. Eliot's 'mystery cat' in *Old Possum's Book of Practical Cats*. Also known as 'The Hidden Paw', the suave but depraved Macavity is 'The Napoleon of Crime'.

MACHIAVELLI — An Italian name appropriate for intelligent male cats. Niccolò Machiavelli was the Italian political theorist, who was author of *The Prince*.

MACINTOSH — For water-loving male cats. The waterproof coat known as the mackintosh was invented in 1823 by Scottish chemist Charles Macintosh.

MADEIRA — A Portuguese name for sweet-natured female cats.

The Madeira islands are an archipelago in the Atlantic well known for sweet Madeira wine.

MADELEINE   A Proustian French name for dainty female cats. In Proust's novel *Remembrance of Things Past*, a bite of a Madeleine biscuit evokes memories of childhood.

MADONNA   A pop-inspired name for energetic female felines. Singer Madonna is noted for her lively stage performances.

MAE   For large, seductive female felines. Actress Mae West was a 1930s sex symbol, starring in films like *She Done Him Wrong*.

MAGRITTE   An artistic name for male cats. René Magritte was a Belgian surrealist painter noted for his serenely dreamlike pictures.

MAJOR   The name given to the poet Stevie Smith's cat, about whom she wrote, 'Major is a fine cat.'

MALCOLM X   A civil rights name for tough black tom-cats. Malcolm X was the radical black American civil rights campaigner.

MALI An African name for cats of either sex. Mali is a West African country.

MALORY For chivalrous male cats. Thomas Malory was the author of the *Morte d'Arthur*, the story of King Arthur.

MALT An old-fashioned name given to the much-loved stripy tom belonging to The Old Woman Who Lived in a Vinegar Bottle in Rumer Godden's eponymous children's tale.

MANCHESTER A city name for urban tom-cats. Manchester, a city in north-west England, grew to prominence during the Industrial Revolution.

MANDARIN A fruit-inspired name for ginger cats of either sex. The orange-skinned mandarin is a member of the citrus family.

MANGO Another fruit-inspired name for sweet-natured ginger cats of either sex. The mango is a tropical fruit with luscious, sweet orange-coloured flesh.

MANX A classic name for tailless or Manx cats. Manx cats, from the Isle of Man, are a breed of short-haired tailless cats rumoured to be descended from cats on the ships of the Spanish Armada.

MAPLE   A tree-inspired name for sweet-natured cats of either sex fond of climbing trees. The sugar maple tree from North America is the source of maple syrup.

MARCO POLO   For adventurous tom-cats given to exploring. Marco Polo was the famous medieval Venetian traveller who entered the court of Kublai Khan and travelled as far as southern India.

MARGATE   A seaside name for water-loving tom-cats. Margate is a well-known British seaside resort.

MARGOT   A balletic name for graceful female cats. Ballet-dancer Margot Fonteyn, famously partnered by Rudolf Nureyev, was noted for her grace and purity of line.

MARIGOLD   A flower-inspired name for ginger female cats. The pot marigold from Europe bears orange or yellow flowers.

MARILYN   A Hollywood name for beautiful female cats.

Film actress Marilyn Monroe, star of films like *Some Like It Hot* and *Gentlemen Prefer Blondes*, was, and remains, a famous sex symbol.

MARLENE For large-eyed fine-boned female felines. Sultrily beautiful German film star Marlene Dietrich starred in films like *Blonde Venus* and *Shanghai Express*.

MARLON A cinema-inspired name for tough tom-cats. Marlon Brando, star of *On the Waterfront* and *The Wild One*, was noted for his brooding screen presence and formidable persona.

MARLOWE A tough masculine name for investigative tom-cats. Moody private eye Marlowe was the hero of Raymond Chandler's famous detective novels. Sixteenth-century dramatist Christopher Marlowe was otherwise known as Kit Marlowe.

MARMADUKE A classic name for marmalade tom-cats.

MARMALADE A domestic name for orange tabbies of either sex. Marmalade is a popular breakfast jam made from oranges.

MARRAKESH   An exotic name for cats of either sex. Marrakesh is the former capital of Morocco, famous for its carpets.

MARSALA   An Italian wine-inspired name for female cats. Marsala wine, named after the Sicilian port, is a sweet wine.

MARSEILLES   A French name for water-loving cats of either sex. Marseilles is France's major seaport.

MARTINIQUE   A tropical name for cats of either sex. The island of Martinique is in the Windward Islands in the West Indies.

MATA HARI   For seductive female cats. Mata Hari was a famous seductive Dutch courtesan who worked as a professional dancer in Paris in 1905.

MATISSE   An artistic name for colourful male cats. French painter Henri Matisse initiated Fauvism at the turn of the nineteenth century and was noted for his vibrantly colourful pictures.

MATTY   Gavin Ewart's 'variegated' black, brown and white cat, immortalized by the poet in *Jubilate Matteo*, which ends 'For I rejoice in my cat, who has the true spirit of Putney'.

MAVERICK   For independent cats of either sex. A maverick is an independent-minded person.

MAX   A dashing name for imperial tom-cats. Max is a variant of Maximilian, the name of a Holy Roman Emperor.

MAY   A spring-inspired name for white-coated female cats, especially those born in the month of May, when white May blossom is in bloom.

MEDEA   A mythic name for strong-willed female cats. The daughter of King Aeetes, she helped Jason steal the Golden Fleece.

MEDICI   An historic name for dominating male cats. The Medici family dominated the Florentine government from 1434 to 1737 and were notable patrons of the Renaissance.

MEEP   The expressive monosyllabic name given to an endearingly mischievous black tom-cat of my acquaintance who's a bit of a buffoon.

MEHITABEL   An evocatively Egyptian name for the most feminine of felines. Mehitabel was immortalized by Archie the New York cockroach in Don Marquis's quirky books about the cat and the cockroach.

MELBA   An operatic name for vocal female felines. Opera singer Dame Nellie Melba was a famous Australian soprano.

MELISSA   A Greek name for sweet-natured female cats. *Melissa* is Greek for 'bee'.

MELODY   A music-inspired name for female cats.

MEPHISTOPHELES   A diabolical name for cunning tom-cats. Mephistopheles was the evil spirit to whom Faust sold his soul in the famous German legend.

MERCURY   A mythic name, appropriate for fast-moving cats. In Roman mythology Mercury was the messenger of the gods, depicted wearing winged sandals.

MERLIN   A wizardly name for wise tom-cats. In Arthurian legend Merlin was the wizard who advised King Arthur.

MICK A rock 'n' roll name for sexy, energetic tom-cats. Rolling Stones singer Mick Jagger, famous for songs like *Satisfaction*, is still strutting his stuff.

MICKEY A Hollywood name for comic, boyish tom-cats. Child actor Mickey Rooney starred opposite Judy Garland as the archetypal American boy next door.

MIDGE For small and energetic cats of either sex. The midge is a tiny harmless insect resembling a mosquito.

MIGNON A French name for dainty female felines. *Mignon* is a French word meaning 'dainty'.

MIKE The simple name given to a beloved cat who lived at the British Museum between 1909 and 1929.

MILAN The stylishly urban name of an energetic, city-dwelling, grey kitten of my acquaintance.

MILES A jazz-inspired name for cool tom-cats. Jazz trumpeter Miles Davis was one of the originators of cool jazz.

MILKY   For white cats of either sex with a partiality for milk.

MILTON   A poetic name for intelligent tom-cats. English poet John Milton was the author of the great epic poem *Paradise Lost*.

MIMOSA   A flower-inspired name for graceful female felines. Mimosa is a feathery-leafed shrub with sweet-scented catkins of yellow flowers.

MING   An elegant name with oriental associations used by Patricia Highsmith in her chilling story *Ming's Biggest Prey*. An especially appropriate name for oriental cats.

MINNALOUSHE   A poetically beautiful, musical name for black cats. It is the name used by Yeats in his poem *The Cat and the Moon* about 'black Minnaloushe'.

MINNELLI   For vocal female felines, inspired by actress and singer Liza Minnelli, star of *Cabaret*.

MINT   A herb-inspired name for green-eyed cats of either sex. Green-leafed mint is a popular herb with a distinctive fragrance.

MISCHIEF   An apt name for mischievous cats of either sex.

MISTER   A masculine name for dignified tom-cats. 'Mister' is a polite form of address for men.

MISTOFELEES   A magical name for clever, small, black tom-cats from T. S. Eliot's *Old Possum's Book of Practical Cats*. Mr Mistofelees is 'The Original Conjuring Cat'.

MISTY   A classic weather-inspired name for grey cats of either sex.

MIZOGUCHI   A Japanese name for oriental male cats. Kenji Mizoguchi was a famous Japanese film director.

MOCHA   An appropriate name for coffee-coloured cats. Mocha is a fine quality coffee named after an Arabian port at the entrance to the Red Sea.

MOG   A down-to-earth cat name for cats of either sex. Mog is a term for an alley-cat, the opposite of a highly bred feline.

MOMMA CASS   The affectionate maternal name given to a dainty American tabby I met in San Francisco who sat sweetly on the rocking chair in the evenings.

MONET
An artistic name for male cats. Claude Monet was the French impressionist painter noted for his landscapes.

MONTEZUMA
The Aztec name for regal male cats. Montezuma was the last Aztec Emperor of Mexico.

MOON
A lunar name for night-loving cats of either sex and especially appropriate for silver-grey cats, whose colour is similar to the light of the moon.

MORDECAI
A Babylonian name for water-loving male cats. In Babylonian mythology Mordecai was the god of water.

MORGAN
A swashbuckling name for piratical tom-cats. In T. S. Eliot's poem gruff-mannered Cat Morgan, now retired from his life on the high seas, is Commissionaire at Faber & Faber.

MOSCOW
A Russian name for city-dwelling tom-cats. Moscow is the capital of Russia.

MOSES
A biblical name for patriarchal male cats. In the Old Testament Moses led his people from slavery in Egypt towards the Promised Land.

MOUSCHI The endearing name given to Anne Frank's cat, who kept her company while she was in hiding from the Nazis.

MOZART A classical name for talented musical cats. Wolfgang Amadeus Mozart was the eighteenth-century Austrian composer who was a child prodigy.

MUDDY A blues name for mellow tom-cats. Musician Muddy Waters was a highly influential bluesman.

MUESLI A food-inspired name for healthy cats of either sex. Muesli is a breakfast food made from cereals, dried nuts and fruit, invited by a Swiss doctor.

MUFFIN A food-inspired name for sweet-natured cats. English and American muffins are both types of cake.

MULBERRY A fruit-inspired name for dark-furred cats of either sex. The dark purple-black mulberry was enjoyed in previous centuries, but is rare nowadays.

MUNGOJERRIE T. S. Eliot's crime-loving cat who with Rumpelteazer forms 'a very notorious couple of cats'.

MUSTARD A spicy name for hot-tempered cats of either sex. Mustard seeds, from which mustard is made, have a distinctive piquancy.

MYRTLE A plant-inspired name for green-eyed female cats. Myrtle is an evergreen shrub with fragrant white flowers.

MYSHKIN The Russian name I gave to my sweet-natured, slightly dim, grey tom-cat. Prince Myshkin is the name of the gentle Holy Fool who is the hero of Dostoevsky's novel *The Idiot*.

NANTUCKET   An American island name for water-loving tom-cats. Nantucket, an island off the east coast of the USA, was traditionally a whaling centre.

NAOMI   A feminine name for lithe, slim felines, inspired by tall, slender supermodel Naomi Campbell.

NAPOLEON   An imperial name for small but formidable tom-cats given to battles. Napoleon I was the highly successful military commander who proclaimed himself Emperor of France in 1804 but was finally defeated at the Battle of Waterloo.

NASHVILLE   An American name for tough, country-loving tom-cats. Nashville, which is the capital of Tennessee, is also the famous centre of country and western music.

NASTASSJA   A film-inspired name for beautiful, slinky female felines. Nastassja Kinski is the beautiful actress who starred in the film *Cat People*.

NATTY　A Hebrew name for male cats given as gifts. Natty is a variant of Nathaniel, which means 'gift of God'.

NEFERTITI　An Egyptian name for elegant female felines. Nefertiti was the chief wife of Akhenaton, Pharaoh of Ancient Egypt.

NELSON　The suitably patriotic and heroic name given to Churchill's wartime headquarters cat. Horatio Nelson was the British admiral who defeated the French and Spanish at Trafalgar in 1805.

NEPTUNE　A mythological name for regal, water-loving tom-cats. In Roman mythology Neptune is the god of the sea, often portrayed holding a trident.

NERO　An Italian name for dominating black male cats. Nero was a Roman Emperor notorious for his cruelty and *nero* is also the Italian for 'black'.

NETTLE　A plant-inspired name for prickly cats of either sex.

NICO   An appropriate name for victorious tom-cats. Nico
is a variant of Nicholas, which derives from the
Greek *nike*, meaning 'victory'.

NIJINSKY   A balletic name for graceful male cats. Vaslav
Nijinsky was a famous Russian ballet dancer who
gained an international reputation with
Diaghilev's dance company.

NIKON   A photography-inspired name for alert, wide-eyed male cats. Nikon cameras are used by professional photographers.

NIMROD   A biblical name for predatory tom-cats. In the biblical Book of Genesis Nimrod is described as a mighty hunter.

NINETTE   A dance-inspired name for graceful female felines. Dame Ninette de Valois is a British ballet dancer and choreographer who founded the Sadler's Wells ballet.

NOËL   The perfect name for suave, assured tom-cats. Songwriter and playwright Noël Coward was noted for his wit and elegance, both in his writing and in his personal life.

NUTMEG   A spice-inspired name for brown-furred cats of either sex. The nutmeg is a brown seed, native to Indonesia, used in both sweet and savoury dishes.

OATS   A food-inspired name for healthy cats of either sex.

ODYSSEUS   A mythological name for intelligent, adventurous tom-cats. Odysseus was a legendary Greek hero, noted for his cunning and courage. He is the hero of Homer's epic poem the *Odyssey*, which charts his adventures journeying home after the Trojan War.

OKRA   A vegetable-inspired name for slender, green-eyed female cats. Okra, also called lady's fingers, is an edible green seed-pod native to Africa.

OLGA   A Russian name for saintly female cats. Olga is a Russian name, derived from the Norse *helga*, meaning 'holy'.

OLIVE   A Mediterranean name for golden-furred female cats. The olive tree has been cultivated for

117

centuries and is highly prized for its fruit, from which golden-green olive oil is derived.

OLIVER A popular name, made famous by a fluffy ginger tom who gained celebrity because he enjoyed being vacuumed by his loving owners!

OLIVIER A thespian name for handsome, aristocratic tom-cats. Dashingly good-looking actor Laurence Olivier was a star of both stage and screen in films like *Henry V* and plays like *The Entertainer*.

OLYMPUS A legendary name for lofty-minded male cats. Mount Olympus in central Greece was thought in ancient times to be the home of the gods.

OMAR A poetic name, especially suitable for Persian tom-cats. Omar Khayyám was a Persian poet, famed for his *Rubayat*.

OPAL A gemstone-inspired name for bright-eyed cats of either sex. The opal is a precious stone noted for its internal play of colours.

ORANGE A fruit-inspired name for ginger felines of either sex. The orange is a popular citrus fruit.

OREGANO   A herb-inspired name for cats of either sex. Oregano is a herb used in Mediterranean cooking.

ORLANDO   The delightfully debonair marmalade-coloured cat who is the star of Kathleen Hale's delightful illustrated series of children's books.

ORSON   A cinematic name for charismatic portly tom-cats. Actor and director Orson Welles directed and starred in *Citizen Kane*.

ORTON   An appropriate name for dramatic tom-cats. Playwright Joe Orton was noted for his black comedies *Loot* and *What the Butler Saw*.

OSCAR   A Hollywood-inspired name for glamorous tom-cats. The Oscars are annual film awards presented by the American Academy of Motion Pictures, Arts and Science.

OTTO   A Germanic name for regal male cats. Otto the Great (912–75) was King of Germany and Holy Roman Emperor.

PALERMO   An Italian name for tough tom-cats. Palermo is
           the capital of Sicily, the Italian island notorious
           for its mafia connections.

PANDORA   A mythological name for alluring female felines.
           In Greek mythology Pandora was the first
           woman. Her dowry was a box containing all the
           world's evils and the consolation of hope.

PANGUR   The name of a monk's white cat immortalized in a
           famous eighth-century poem by an unknown
           author.

PANTHER   A suitable name for large black cats. The panther
           is a type of leopard with black pigmentation.

PAPAYA   A fruit-inspired name for ginger-furred cats of
           either sex. The papaya is an orange-skinned
           tropical fruit.

PAPRIKA A spice-inspired name for fiery-natured female felines. Paprika, a member of the capsicum family, is a slightly piquant spice.

PAPYRUS An Egyptian name for slender cats of either sex. Papyrus is a reed-like plant, cultivated by the Ancient Egyptians for its use as paper.

PARIS The French name of my chic, black, city-dwelling cat, suggested by France's capital rather than the Greek hero.

PARKER An apt name for rhythmic tom-cats or sharp-witted female felines. Charlie Parker, also known as 'Bird', was a notable jazz saxophonist and composer, while Dorothy Parker was a famous witty twentieth-century American author.

PARMA An Italian name for female cats partial to ham. Parma ham is a famous Italian salt-cured ham.

PARSLEY After Parsley the Lion from the children's TV series *The Herb Garden*.

PATCH A much-loved name for patchwork cats of either sex.

PAVAROTTI An opera-inspired name for vocal, portly tom-cats. Luciano Pavarotti is a noted Italian operatic tenor.

PAVLOVA A ballet name for graceful female felines. Anna Pavlova was a famous Russian ballet dancer who created the chief role in *Les Sylphides*.

PEACH A fruit-inspired name for soft-furred female cats.

PEACOCK For beautiful but vain male cats. The peacock is a flamboyantly feathered male bird, traditionally thought to be vain.

PEANUTS A cartoon-inspired name for comic tom-cats. *Peanuts* is an American cartoon-strip featuring the philosophical dog Snoopy.

PEARL A jewel-inspired name for beautiful white female cats. Pearls are formed in oysters around grains of sand and are prized for their lustre.

PECAN A nut-inspired name for brown-furred cats of either sex. The brown pecan nut, from a variety of hickory tree, is especially popular in America.

PEKING A Chinese name, especially appropriate for oriental cats. Peking is the capital city of China.

PELE A football-inspired name for speedy, athletic tom-cats. Pele was a great Brazilian footballer who scored over 1,300 goals.

PENELOPE A poetic name for intelligent female felines. In Greek mythology Penelope was the wife of Odysseus who ingeniously managed to keep her suitors at bay while her husband returned from the Trojan War.

PEONY A flower-inspired name for female cats, especially suitable for oriental cats. The peony flower is prized in China and is often depicted in paintings and drawings.

PEPPER A spice-inspired name for fiery cats of either sex. Pepper is a spice derived from the fruits of a climbing vine. It has a distinctive hot flavour.

PEPPERMINT A sweet-inspired name for cats of either sex, especially appropriate for white cats.

PEPSI   An American name for lively male cats. Pepsi-cola is a popular sugar-rich drink, thought to give energy.

PEPYS   A literary name for inquisitive male cats. Samuel Pepys was a famous English diarist, noted for his curiosity.

PERCY   A poetic name for courtly male cats. Sir Perceval was a pure-spirited knight in Arthurian legend while Percy Bysshe Shelley was a leading poet of the Romantic movement.

PERICLES   A Greek name for stately male cats. Pericles was an Athenian statesman noted for his oratory and honesty.

PERSEPHONE   A mythological name for desirable female cats. In Greek mythology Persephone, daughter of Demeter, was abducted by Hades and forced to spend six months each year in his underworld.

PERSEUS   A mythological name for heroic male cats. In Greek mythology Perseus overcame Medusa, who turned men to stone.

PERSIA An exotic name, particularly suitable for Persian cats. Persia, now Iran, is an ancient Middle Eastern country.

PERSIMMON A fruit-inspired name for ginger-coloured cats of both sexes. The persimmon is a sweet-fleshed, orange-skinned fruit.

PERU A South American name for male cats. The country of Peru is the former home of the Incas.

PETER The name of poet Marianne Moore's cat 'who sleeps his time away'.

PHARAOH An Egyptian name for regal male cats. Pharaoh was the title of ancient Egyptian rulers, deriving from the Egyptian for 'great house'.

PHOENIX A legendary name for golden-furred, sun-loving cats of either sex. The phoenix is a fabulous golden bird associated with sun-worship.

PIAF For small, strong-willed, vocal female cats. The French cabaret singer Edith Piaf's small size earned her the nickname *Piaf*, meaning 'Sparrow'.

PICASSO An artistic name for energetic male cats. Spanish artist Pablo Picasso was a developer of Cubism and noted for his prodigious energy and creativity.

PICCOLO An Italian name for small male cats. *Piccolo* is Italian for 'small'. *Piccola* is the female version.

PICKLES A food-inspired name for cats of either sex.

PILCHARD   For fish-loving cats of either sex. The pilchard is a
            type of fish related to the herring and the sprat.

PINEAPPLE   A fruit-inspired name for sharp-clawed cats of
            either sex. The tropical pineapple fruit is protected
            by a thick, spiky skin.

PIRANHA   For sharp-toothed cats of either sex. The piranha
            is a South American fish notorious for its razor-
            sharp teeth.

PISTACHIO   A nut-inspired name for green-eyed cats of either
            sex. The pistachio is a green-coloured nut with a
            distinctive flavour.

PIZZA   A food-inspired name for speedy cats of either
            sex. Italian pizza has become a popular fast food.

PLATO   A Greek name for philosophical tom-cats. Plato
            was an Athenian philosopher and a devoted fol-
            lower of Socrates.

PLUM   A literary name for comic male cats. It was the
            nickname of humorous writer P. G. Wodehouse,
            author of the classic Jeeves and Bertie Wooster
            books.

PLUTO A name with distinct underworld connotations. It is the name given to the sagacious feline in Edgar Allan Poe's macabre story *The Black Cat*.

POLKA A dance-inspired name for lively cats of either sex. The polka was a Bohemian folk dance which became a popular ballroom dance in the nineteenth century.

POLLOCK For artistic male cats. American artist Jackson Pollock developed a distinctive abstract style.

POLO A mint-inspired name for white cats of either sex. 'The mint with a hole' is a popular sweet.

POMEGRANATE A fruit-inspired name for sweet-natured cats. The pomegranate, with its juicy, sweet seeds, is grown in tropical and sub-tropical countries.

POMPADOUR A French name for elegant female felines. Madame de Pompadour was the influential mistress of Louis XV and a patron of the arts.

POMPEY A Roman name for combative tom-cats. Pompey was a Roman general who fought against Julius Caesar and was defeated at Pharsalus.

POPCORN A snack-inspired name for casual cats of either sex. Popcorn is a snack-food, eaten especially at the cinema.

POPEYE A cartoon name for tough tom-cats. Popeye the sailor man is a muscular, spinach-eating cartoon character.

POPPY A flower-inspired name for tranquil female felines. The seeds of the opium poppy were used as a tranquillizing opiate.

PORTHOS A French name for greedy and portly tom-cats. Porthos was the food-loving musketeer in Dumas's swashbuckling novel *The Three Musketeers*.

PRESLEY A rock 'n' roll cat for cool tom-cats. Singer Elvis Presley, whose hits included *Heartbreak Hotel* and *Hound Dog*, was the King of Rock 'n' Roll.

PRIMROSE A flower-inspired name for dainty female cats. The primrose is a delicate, pale yellow flower, found in hedgerows and woodlands.

PRINCE A pop-inspired name for small, sexy cats. The

artist formerly known as Prince is noted for his charisma and his small stature.

PROVENCE   A French name for rural cats of either sex. Provence is a region of France noted for its beautiful, fertile countryside.

PRUNE   A fruit-inspired name for black-furred cats of either sex. Prunes are dried plums.

PUCCINI   An operatic name for vocal male cats. Giacomo Puccini was an Italian opera composer, whose works included *Tosca* and *Turandot*.

PUDDING   An affectionately humorous name for fat tom-cats.

PUFFBALL   A mushroom-inspired name appropriate for large white fluffy cats. Puffball is a giant, globular fungi which may reach over 3.5ft (1 metre) across.

PUFFIN   A bird-inspired name for black-and-white cats of either sex. The puffin is a north Atlantic seabird with distinctive black-and-white markings.

PUMPERNICKEL A German name for brown-furred cats of either sex. Pumpernickel is a German wholemeal rye bread.

PUMPKIN A vegetable-inspired name for plump tom-cats. The pumpkin is a large round vegetable.

PURRBALL An affectionate name for purry cats of either sex.

PURRY A classic name for purry cats of either sex.

PUSHKIN A poetic Russian name for male cats. Alexander Pushkin was a Russian poet and dramatist, author of the epic verse novel *Eugene Onegin*.

PUSS The classic name for either male or female felines. It is the name given to the dashing cat in Charles Perrault's fairy-tale *Puss in Boots*.

PUSSY A popular name for felines of either sex. Edward Lear's poem *The Owl and the Pussycat* contains a very feminine feline.

PYRAMID An Egyptian name for monumental male cats.

QUARTZ   A crystalline name for bright-eyed cats of either sex. Coloured varieties of quartzes include purple amethyst and pink rose quartz.

QUEENIE   A regal name for female cats. Queenie is a variant of Queen.

QUENTIN   An old-fashioned name for male cats, especially appropriate for the fifth kitten in a brood. The name comes from the Roman *quintus*, meaning 'fifth'.

QUINCE   A fruit-inspired name for yellow-furred female cats. The quince is a golden yellow-skinned pear-shaped fruit.

RA   An Ancient Egyptian name for lordly male cats. Ra was the Egyptian sun god and lord of creation.

RADISH   A vegetable-inspired name for garden-loving cats of either sex.

RAFFLES   A literary name for stealthy male cats. Raffles was the name of the famous fictional gentleman cat burglar.

RALEGH   A dashing name for intrepid tom-cats given to exploring. Sir Walter Ralegh was the famous Elizabethan explorer who brought back the potato and tobacco plants from America.

RAMA   An Indian name for heroic male cats. In Indian mythology Rama is the seventh incarnation of Vishnu, appearing as a hero in the epics the *Ramayana* and *Mahabharata*.

RANGIE — The name given to a handsome long-legged Burmese cat of my acquaintance.

RANGOON — An exotic name, especially apt for Burmese cats. Rangoon is the capital of Burma.

RAPHAEL — An artistic name for angelic male cats. Raphael was an Italian Renaissance painter noted for his depiction of the Madonna.

RASPBERRY — A fruit-inspired name for sweet cats of either sex.

RASPINI — An Italian name for elegant male felines. Raspini is an Italian shoe shop noted for the quality of its leather.

RATATOUILLE — A food-inspired name for sun-loving cats of either sex. Ratatouille is a Mediterranean dish made using aubergines, tomatoes and courgettes, evocative of sunny climates.

RAYMOND — An old-fashioned name for male cats.

REX — An appropriate name for regal male cats, especially suitable for Rex cats. *Rex* is Latin for 'king'.

REYNARD   An old-fashioned name for ginger-coated tom-cats. In the satirical medieval epic *Reynard the Fox*, the ginger-coated fox is the cunning hero.

RHODES   A Greek name for water-loving male cats. Rhodes is a Greek island in the Aegean Sea, the largest of the Dodecanese group.

RICHELIEU   A French name for cunning male cats. Cardinal Richelieu was a French statesman noted for his ruthlessness.

RITA   A Hollywood name for beautiful female felines. Glamorous film star Rita Hayworth starred in movies including *Gilda* and *Cover Girl*.

RITZ   A hotel-inspired name for elegant male cats. The Ritz on Piccadilly is a prestigious London hotel.

ROBIN   A legendary name for adventurous male cats with a penchant for climbing trees. Robin Hood was the legendary medieval forest-dwelling outlaw, noted for his daring, who stole from the rich to give to the poor.

ROBINSON   A literary name for solitary male cats. Robinson

Crusoe, the hero of Defoe's eponymous novel, finds himself shipwrecked and alone on a desert island.

ROCKET For energetic cats of either sex.

ROCKY For tough tom-cats with a predilection for fights. Sylvester Stallone starred as a down-on-his-luck boxer in the popular film *Rocky*.

ROLEX A jet-set name for sleek tom-cats. Rolex watches are an expensive status symbol.

ROLLO An old-fashioned name for warrior tom-cats. Rollo is a variant of Roland, who was the chivalrous warrior immortalized in the medieval *Song of Roland*.

ROLO A confectionery-inspired name for sweet cats of either sex. The Rolo is a popular chocolate-coated toffee.

ROMA An Italian name for cosmopolitan cats of either sex. Roma, or Rome in English, is the Italian capital city, famous for its style and flair.

ROSETTA   For enigmatic female cats. The Rosetta Stone is an
           inscribed stone slab with a hieroglyphic inscrip-
           tion which baffled interpretation for decades.

ROSSINI   An operatic name for vocal male cats. Gioacchino
           Rossini was an Italian composer whose operas
           included *The Barber of Seville* and *The Thieving
           Magpie*.

ROUSSEAU   A French name for free-spirited tom-cats. Jean-
           Jacques Rousseau was an eighteenth-century
           philosopher famous for his theory of the 'noble
           savage'.

RUBY   A gem-inspired name for precious female cats.
           The ruby is a red gemstone, a variety of corun-
           dum.

RUDOLF   A balletic name for graceful male cats. Rudolf
           Nureyev was a Russian ballet dancer who part-
           nered Margot Fonteyn and was famous for his
           agility, charisma and technique.

RUDYARD   An Old Saxon name for solitary male cats. It is
           inspired by writer and poet Rudyard Kipling,
           author of *The Cat Who Walks Alone*.

RUM TUM   The perverse tom-cat immortalized by T. S. Eliot
            in *Old Possum's Book of Practical Cats*: 'The Rum
            Tum Tugger is a Curious Cat: If you offer him
            pheasant he would rather have grouse.'

RUMPELTEAZER The name of T. S. Eliot's cat burglar, partner in
            crime with Mungojerrie.

RUMPUSCAT   T. S. Eliot's great fearsome feline. In Eliot's poem
            The Battle of the Pekes and the Pollicles, the 'Great
            Rumpuscat', with his fireball eyes and amazing
            jaws puts a rapid end to the conflict.

RUNCIBLE   The Edward Lear-derived name given to a large
            tabby farm-cat I know of who helps his owner
            round up the sheep.

RUSKIN   A literary name for thoughtful male cats. John
            Ruskin was an influential Victorian art critic, the
            author of *Modern Painters*.

SACHA   For suave male cats with a penchant for crooning. Sacha is the name of a famous male crooner.

SAFFRON   A spice-inspired name for costly cats of either sex. Saffron, made from crocus stamens, is the most costly spice in the world.

SAGE   A herb-inspired name for grey cats of either sex. Sage, a grey-leafed herb, has a strong distinctive flavour.

SAGITTARIUS   A zodiac-inspired name for cats with a flair for hunting born between 22 November and 22 December.

SAGO   A food-inspired name, suitable for cats of either sex. Sago is a starchy food derived from sago palms.

SAHA   A literary name for elegant female felines. Saha is the feline protagonist of Colette's classic story *The Cat*.

SAKE   A Japanese name for male or female cats, especially appropriate for oriental cats. Sake is the potent Japanese rice wine traditionally drunk warm.

SAKI   A literary name for elegant tom-cats with sharp claws. Saki was the pen-name of H. H. Munro, witty author of *Tobermory*, a story about a cat with the power of speech.

SALMON   For fish-loving cats of either sex. The salmon is prized as the king of fish.

SALSA   A Latino name for nimble cats of either sex. The salsa is a type of Latin American dance.

SAM   A down-to-earth name belonging to a handsome black cat of my acquaintance.

SAMBA   A musical name for rhythmic cats. The samba is a type of dance.

SAMBAL   A chilli-inspired name for fiery cats of either sex. In Malay cooking sambal is a chilli condiment.

SAMUEL   A literary name for humorous tom-cats. Cat-loving American author Samuel Langhorne Clemens, author of *Tom Sawyer* and *Huckleberry Finn*, was better known as Mark Twain.

SANTAYANA   A Spanish name for philosophical male cats. George Santayana was a Spanish-born philosopher and poet.

SAPPHIRE   A gem-inspired name, suitable for blue-eyed cats of either sex.

SAPPHO   A literary name for passionate female cats. Sappho was a Greek literary poet, famous for her poems written for her group of female admirers on the island of Lesbos.

SARDINE   A piscine name for fish-loving cats of either sex.

SARK   An island-inspired name for independent male cats. Sark is one of the Channel Islands, which is governed by its own hereditary seigneur or dame in a semi-feudal system.

SAVILE An elegant name for distinguished male cats. Savile Row is a London street, famous for its bespoke tailors.

SAVOY A hotel-inspired name for elegant cats of either sex. The Savoy hotel in London's Strand is a world-famous establishment.

SCALA An opera-inspired name for vocal female felines. La Scala is a world-famous opera house in Milan.

SCARLETT A literary name for beautiful and demanding female felines. Scarlett O'Hara is the name of Margaret Mitchell's tempestuous heroine in *Gone With the Wind*, embodied by Vivien Leigh in the film of the novel.

SCONE A cake-inspired name for domestic cats of both sexes. Scones are a classic English tea-time treat.

SCORPIO A zodiac-inspired name for cats born between 23 October and 21 November.

SCOTT A literary name for suavely elegant male cats. American author F. Scott Fitzgerald portrayed

1920s high society life in novels like *The Great Gatsby* and *Tender is the Night*.

SCOTTIE A *Star Trek*-inspired name for earnest male cats. Scottie is the Scottish doctor on the Starship *Enterprise*.

SCRABBLE A game-inspired name for intelligent cats of either sex. Scrabble is an enormously popular word board game.

SCROOGE A Dickens-inspired name for churlish male cats. In Dickens' story *A Christmas Carol*, Scrooge is a notorious miser who undergoes a seasonal transformation.

SEBASTIAN A Greek name for venerable male cats. Sebastian comes from the Greek for 'venerable'.

SELINA A dainty, feminine name given to the cat in Thomas Gray's poem 'On a favourite Cat, call'd Selina, that fell into a China Tub with Gold-Fishes in it & was drown'd'.

SEMOLINA A food-inspired name for female cats. Semolina is fine grains of durum wheat, used to make pasta.

SERAPHINA   An ancient name for angelic female cats. In the Bible Seraphim were the first order of angels.

SESAME   A seed-inspired name for nutty male or female cats. Sesame seeds are valued for their edible oil with its nutty flavour.

SEVILLE   A Spanish name for marmalade-coloured cats of either sex. Spanish Seville oranges, with their slightly bitter flavour, are used to make mamalade.

SHALLOT   A vegetable-inspired name for cats of either sex. Shallots are members of the garlic family with a mild onion flavour.

SHANDY   A drink-inspired name for mild cats of either sex. Shandy is made by mixing beer or lager with lemonade to create a mildly alcoholic drink.

SHEBA   A feminine name for queenly felines. The Queen of Sheba was famous for her dazzling beauty and wit and is reputed to have seduced King Solomon.

SHELLEY   A poetic name for rebellious male cats. Percy

Bysshe Shelley was a revolutionary young poet of the Romantic movement, author of *Ode to the West Wind*.

SHERE KHAN   A literary name for ferocious striped male cats. In Kipling's *Jungle Book*, Shere Khan is the savage, man-hunting tiger who threatens Mowgli.

SHERLOCK   A literary name for intelligent, inquisitive male cats. Sherlock Holmes is the famous Victorian detective created by Sir Arthur Conan Doyle.

SHERRY   A drink-inspired name for golden-brown cats of either sex. Sherry is a Spanish fortified wine with a varying pale or deep golden colour.

SIAM   An exotic name and an obvious choice for Siamese cats of either sex. Siam was Thailand's ancient name.

SIBELIUS   A musical name for tom-cats. Jean Sibelius was a Finnish composer, famous for *Finlandia*.

SIBYL   A mythological name for wise female cats. In Greek and Roman mythology the sibyls were divinely inspired prophetesses.

SICILY An Italian-inspired name for sun-loving cats of either sex. Sicily is a Mediterranean island off the Italian coast with a warm, sunny climate.

SIEGFRIED A Germanic name for heroic tom-cats. In German legend Siegfried is a heroic warrior.

SIGMUND A psychiatric name for thoughtful male cats. Austrian psychiatrist Sigmund Freud was a pioneer of psychoanalysis.

SILVER A metal-inspired name for grey male or female cats.

SILVESTER An apt name for saintly male cats. In legend Saint Silvester baptized Emperor Constantine.

SIMON A masculine name for intrepid tom-cats. It is the name of a heroic black-and-white tom-cat whose WWII naval career earned him the animal VC.

SINATRA For vocal blue-eyed tom-cats. Singer Frank Sinatra, known as Ol' Blue Eyes, is famous for songs such as *Strangers in the Night* and *My Way*.

SINBAD A literary name for tom-cats who enjoy exploring, inspired by Sinbad the Sailor, a heroic character from the Arabian tales *A Thousand and One Nights*.

SIR JOHN LANGBORN
The distinguished name given to the English writer Jeremy Bentham's cat, of whom he wrote, 'He gradually obtained a great reputation for sanctity and learning and a Doctor's degree was conferred upon him.'

SISLEY
An artistic name for male cats. Alfred Sisley was an Impressionist painter noted for his landscapes.

SKIMBLESHANKS
T. S. Eliot's green-eyed 'railway cat' from *Old Possum's Book of Practical Cats*: 'He gives you a wave of his long brown tail/Which says: I'll see you again!/You'll meet without fail on the Midnight Mail/the Cat of the Railway Train.'

SKIPPER
A nautical name for commanding tom-cats with a taste for the ocean waves. Skipper is the title given to the captain of a boat.

SKITTER
The appropriate name given by my father to a very pretty but nervy white cat who lived in a Tuscan farmhouse.

SLIPPERS The affectionate, down-to-earth name given to Mrs Theodore Roosevelt's grey, six-toed White House cat in 1906.

SMARTIE A confectionery-inspired name for multi-coloured sweet-natured cats of either sex.

SMOKEY A classic name for grey cats of either sex.

SMUDGE An apt name for cats with patchwork markings.

SNOWBALL An appropriate name for rotund white cats of either sex, inspired by white snow.

SNOWDROP The dainty name given to Alice's white kitten in *Alice Through the Looking Glass*.

SNOWFLAKE A popular name for female white cats, inspired by white snow.

SNOWY A classic name for white cats of either sex, inspired by white snow.

SOCKS President Clinton's cat, currently resident at the White House and very popular with the journalistic rat-pack.

SOCRATES A Greek name for philosophical tom-cats. Socrates was an Athenian philosopher who inspired Plato and Xenophon.

SOLOMON A regal name for wise tom-cats. In the Old Testament Solomon was a King of Israel famed for his wisdom.

SONNY For rhythmic tom-cats, after musician Sonny Rollins.

SOOTY Perennially popular name for black cats of either sex. Soot is the black residue found in chimneys.

SOPHIA For beautiful, large-eyed female felines. Voluptuous Italian actress Sophia Loren starred in films including *Two Women* and *The Millionairess*.

SOPHOCLES A Greek name for dramatic male cats. Sophocles was an Athenian playwright, author of *Oedipus Rex* and *Antigone*.

SOPWITH An aeronautical name for tom-cats with a penchant for heights. The Sopwith Camel was an early plane.

SORREL A plant-inspired name for cats of either sex. Sorrel's tangy leaves are used in salads and soups.

SOYA For healthy female cats. Soya beans are an important source of vegetarian protein used to make beancurd and soy milk.

SPARTACUS A heroic and noble name for rugged tom-cats. Spartacus was a Thracian gladiator who led a slave revolt against Rome in 73 BC.

SPATS A footwear-inspired name for elegant male cats with white or black paws.

SPHINX A legendary name for enigmatic female felines. In Greek mythology the Sphinx killed travellers who could not answer her riddle until it was solved by Oedipus.

SPICE An aromatic name for sweet-smelling male or female cats.

SPICIOLI From the Italian for 'small change', this was the name given to my first cat – a tiny, characterful and elusive black-and-white cat.

SPIKE   A down-to-earth name for tough tom-cats with sharp claws.

SPITFIRE For fiery-tempered cats inclined to spitting.

SPOCK   A *Star Trek*-inspired name for pointy-eared, enigmatic, intelligent male cats. Spock is the superintelligent half-Vulcan half-human who is Captain Kirk's loyal lieutenant on the Starship *Enterprise*.

SQUIRREL The name given to a tiny grey cat I knew with a dominating personality.

STEED   An Avenger-inspired name for dapper black tomcats. Umbrella-toting, bowler-hatted Steed was an unflappable member of the Avengers.

STEINBECK A literary name for tough tom-cats. John Steinbeck was the author of great gritty novels like *The Grapes of Wrath*.

STELLA   A heavenly name for night-loving female cats. *Stella* is Latin for 'star'.

STEVIE   A literary name for quirky female felines. Poetess Stevie Smith was a lover of cats.

STRAWBERRY   A fruit-inspired name for sweet-natured cats of either sex.

STUD   A butch name for virile male cats.

SUEDE   A leather-inspired name for soft-furred cats of either sex.

SUGAR   For sweet-natured female felines, inspired by the popular sweetener.

SUKI   An old-fashioned feminine name for country-living cats.

SUMATRA   An exotic name for cats of either sex. Sumatra is an Indonesian island which produces coffee, tea and pepper.

SUNFLOWER   A flower-inspired name, especially suitable for ginger cats of either sex. The sunflower famously inspired the painter Van Gogh.

SUSHI   A Japanese name for fish-loving felines of either sex. Sushi is a traditional Japanese dish of rice and seaweed wrapped around slivers of raw fish and pickle.

SUSIE A feminine name for dainty female cats. Susie is a variant of Susan, which comes from the Hebrew for 'lily'.

SUSSEX An English name suitable for rural male cats. Sussex is a south-eastern country noted for its downs.

SVENGALI A literary name for intelligent manipulative cats. Svengali is the mysterious, manipulative figure in George du Maurier's novel *Trilby*.

SWEETIE An affectionate name for sweet-natured cats of either sex.

SYLVESTER A masculine name, belonging to the daft black-and-white cartoon cat forever pursuing Tweetiepie.

TABASCO   A food-inspired name for fiery-tempered tom-
           cats. Tabasco sauce is a popular American pepper
           sauce.

TABBY   A classic name for tabby cats of either sex.

TABITHA   A popular name for female tabby cats. A pussycat
           called Tabitha became 'the most famous airborne
           kitty' when she disappeared from her cage on a
           Boeing 747 flight to Los Angeles and spent almost
           two weeks in a state of perpetual transit.

TAHITI   A tropical name for graceful female cats. The
           Polynesian island of Tahiti is famous for its beauti-
           ful scenery and inspired the artist Gauguin.

TALISMAN   For lucky cats of either sex. A talisman is a
           charm or amulet thought to bring its owner good
           fortune.

154

TALLULAH   A glamorous name for slinky female cats. Elegant actress Tallulah Bankhead was a famous star.

TAMARIND   A fruit-inspired name for plump female cats. Bitter-sweet tamarind pulp is used to flavour chutneys and curries.

TAMMANY   The name given by American humorist Mark Twain to one of his cats who he called 'the most beautiful cat on the western bulge of the globe and perhaps the most gifted'.

TANG   An ancient Chinese name, especially suitable for oriental cats. The Tang dynasty lasted from AD 618–906, establishing a Central Asian empire.

TANGERINE   A fruit-inspired name for ginger-furred felines of either sex.

TANGO   A dance-inspired name for seductive felines. The tango is a South American ballroom dance noted for its erotic charge.

TANSY   A herbal name for ginger-coloured female felines. The bitter leaves of the yellow-flowered tansy were used in medicine and cookery.

TAO A Chinese name for contemplative cats of either sex, especially suitable for oriental cats. The concept of Tao, 'the Way', is central to the Chinese philosophy of Taoism.

TARRAGON A herb-inspired name for green-eyed cats of either sex. Tarragon is a fragrant green-leafed herb.

TARTAN A Scottish name for clannish cats of either sex.

TEABAG The rather domestic name given to a cat living in American academic Camille Paglia's apartment block.

TEDDY An American name for presidential male cats. American President Teddy Roosevelt was a great lover of cats.

TENNYSON A literary name for dignified tom-cats. Lord Alfred Tennyson, author of *In Memoriam*, was a Grand Old Man of Victorian poetry.

TENZING A good name for athletic cats who climb up curtains, inspired by the famous sherpa Norgay Tenzing who reached the summit of Mount

Everest in 1953. The variant Tensingh was the name given to the most handsome Siamese of my acquaintance, prompted by his climbing prowess as a kitten.

TEQUILA   A Mexican name for spirited female cats. Tequila is a potent Mexican spirit.

TERRACOTTA   An Italian name especially suitable for reddish-brown female cats. *Terracotta*, which means 'cooked earth', is the name of a reddish fired clay used to make pots and tiles.

TEXAS   An American name for large male cats. Texas is America's second largest state.

THE MASTER'S CAT   The name given by Charles Dickens' servants to the household cat who adored the Victorian author and would follow him about like a dog.

THEO   A distinguished Greek name for patriarchal male cats. Theo comes from the Greek *Theos*, meaning 'God'.

THISTLE   For sharp-clawed cats of either sex. The thistle plant is noted for its sharp prickles.

THOMAS   A classic name for saintly tom-cats. Thomas à Becket was a famous Christian martyr while Thomas Aquinas was a noted theologian.

THOMPSON   For muscular, speedy male cats. Daley Thompson is an Olympic gold-winning decathlete.

THYME   A herb-inspired name for fragrant cats of either sex. Thyme is a popular herb with a distinctive scent.

TIDDLES   A very popular English cat name, used for cats of either sex. The word affectionately implies something diminutive.

TIFFANY   A glamorous name for bright-eyed female cats. Tiffany is the name of a prestigious New York jewellery shop noted for its gems.

TIFFIN   An Indian-inspired name for greedy cats of either sex. Tiffin is the Indian name for a light lunch.

TIGER   Artist Gwen John's name for her beloved cat. An appropriate name for striped cats of either sex.

TIGGER   A literary name for lively, stripy felines. It is the name given by A. A. Milne to the bouncily exuberant tiger in the Winnie the Pooh books.

TINA   A pop name for energetic, vocal female felines. Singer Tina Turner is noted for her on-stage energy.

TIPPI   A Hollywood name for enigmatic female felines. Actress Tippi Hedren, who starred in Hitchcock's *Marnie* and *The Birds,* was noted for her cool blonde screen persona.

TIPSY   A drink-inspired name for thirsty cats of either sex.

TITAN   A mythological name for large tom-cats. In Greek mythology the Titans were gigantic primeval gods and goddesses overthrown by Zeus.

TITIAN An artistic name for ginger-coloured male cats. The Venetian artist Titian was noted for his penchant for red-headed female models.

TITUS   A Shakespearean name for strong rebellious tom-cats, inspired by Shakespeare's play *Titus Andronicus.*

TIVOLI An Italian name for sun-loving cats of either sex. The town of Tivoli was a popular summer resort in Roman times.

TOBAGO A tropical name for laid-back male cats. The West Indian island of Tobago is a popular holiday resort.

TOBERMORY A literary name for intelligent tom-cats. Tobermory is the wickedly observant cat in Saki's witty, eponymous tale of a feline with the gift of speech.

TOBLERONE A confectionery-inspired name for brown-furred male cats suggested by the Toblerone chocolate bar.

TOBY A medieval name for well-behaved tom-cats. Toby is a variant of the Hebrew name Tobias, meaning 'God is good.'

TOFFEE A sweet-inspired name for caramel-coloured cats of either sex.

TOKYO A Japanese name for city-dwelling cats of either sex. Tokyo is the capital city of Japan.

TOLEDO A Spanish name for sharp-clawed tom-cats. Toledo is a Spanish town once famous for its swords.

TOLLIVER An old-fashioned masculine name for tom-cats.

TOLSTOY A distinguished literary name for impressive male cats. Leo Nikolaevich Tolstoy, the author of *War and Peace*, was a great Russian writer.

TOM A popular cat's name often punningly given to tom-cats. Paul Gallico wrote *The Ballad of Tough Tom* which contains the lines: 'My name is Tough Tom/And I am King of the Car-Park.'

TOM KITTEN Beatrix Potter's famous fictional cheeky kitten.

TOM QUARTZ The name given by President Theodore Roosevelt to his 'cunningest kitten'.

TOMATO The plant-inspired name for plump cats of either sex. The tomato is a fleshy red fruit eaten as a vegetable.

TOOTSIE An irreverent name for female cats, especially suitable for fluffy, long-haired cats.

TOP CAT   For charismatic, smart, city-dwelling tom-cats.
Top Cat was the quick-witted leader of a gang of
alley-cats in an eponymous TV cartoon series.

TOPAZ   A gem-inspired name for golden-eyed cats of
either sex. The topaz is a yellow gemstone, the
birthstone of those born in November.

TORINO   An Italian name for urban male cats. Torino,
called Turin in English, is a sophisticated north
Italian town with an intellectual reputation.

TORTOISE   The name of a tortoiseshell tabby in George Eliot's
novel *Middlemarch*. An appropriate name for
tortoiseshell cats and for slow-moving felines.

TOULOUSE   An artistic French name for fun-loving tom-cats.
Artist Toulouse-Lautrec was noted for his paintings of music halls and cafés.

TRAPEZE   A circus-inspired name for acrobatic cats of either
sex with a good head for heights.

TREACLE   For sweet-natured black cats of either sex.

TRILBY   A literary name for dainty female cats or a hat-inspired name for dapper male cats. Trilby was the heroine of George du Maurier's novel *Trilby* and is also the name of a stylish narrow-brimmed felt hat.

TRINIDAD   A Caribbean name for exotic female cats. Trinidad is a West Indian country off South America.

TRISTAN   An Arthurian name for handsome, romantic tom-cats. In medieval romances Tristan becomes the doomed lover of Isolde, who is betrothed to his uncle.

TROMBONE   A musical name for vocal male cats.

TROTSKY   A Russian name for bolshie male cats. Leon Trotsky was a Russian revolutionary and Marxist theorist who was actively involved in Russia's 1918 Bolshevik Revolution.

TROTWOOD   The name given to a male tabby, after Dickens's character Betsey Trotwood, as it was initially thought to be female and called Betsey!

TROY   A legendary name for noble male cats. In ancient legend the Trojan prince Paris abducted the beautiful Helen, leading to the Trojan War against the Greeks.

TRUFFAUT A film-inspired name for stylish tom-cats. François Truffaut was a French film director whose films were noted for their sophisticated charm, e.g. *Jules et Jim*.

TRUFFLE A food-inspired name for greedy tom-cats. The truffle is a distinctively-scented fungus, regarded as a great delicacy.

TRUMPET A music-inspired name for vocal cats of either sex.

TUCKER A jolly name for tom-cats who enjoy their grub. 'Tuck' is a slang word for food, as in 'tuck-boxes'.

TULIP A flower-inspired name for female cats.

TUNA A piscine name for fish-loving female felines.

TUNIS An exotic name for cats of either sex. Tunis is the capital of Tunisia.

TUPPENCE The name given a sweet-natured, grey tom-cat of mine.

TURMERIC   A spice-inspired name for yellow-furred cats of either sex. Turmeric is a spice which gives food a distinctive yellow tinge.

TURNIP   A vegetable-inspired name for down-to-earth cats of either sex.

TURPIN   A good name for bandit cats. Highwayman Dick Turpin is famous for his apocryphal ride from London to York on his faithful horse Black Bess.

TURQUOISE   A stone-inspired name for blue-eyed cats of either sex. Turquoise is a pale blue/green colour and gemstone.

TUSCANY   An Italian name for male cats. Tuscany is a picturesque region of Italy noted for its beautiful landscape.

TUTANKHAMEN   An Egyptian name for regal male cats. Tutankhamen was an Egyptian boy-king who became ruler at the age of 11.

TWAIN   A literary name for lively tom-cats, inspired by cat-loving American humorist Mark Twain, author of *Tom Sawyer* and *Huckleberry Finn*.

TWINKLE   A name given to a huge, fluffy white cat of my
           acquaintance who always looked distinctly belli-
           cose, no doubt reacting against the soppiness of
           her name.

TWITCHET   A dainty, feminine name given to a pretty
           tortoiseshell belonging to my cousins because of
           her sensitive white whiskers.

TYSON   An appropriate name for tough tom-cats. Boxer
           Mike Tyson became the youngest ever world
           heavyweight champion in 1986.

UHURA A TV-inspired name for elegant female felines. Lieutenant Uhura was the glamorous *Star Trek* communications officer.

ULYSSES A legendary name for brave, shrewd tom-cats. Ulysses is another name for Odysseus, the legendary Greek king, whose adventures were told in Homer's *Odyssey*.

UMBERTO A literary Italian name for super-intelligent tom-cats. Umberto Eco is an acclaimed Italian author and academic, author of the best-selling *The Name of the Rose* and *Foucault's Pendulum*.

VALENCIA A Spanish name for female cats. Valencia is a Spanish city, formerly a Moorish capital.

VALENTINO A romantic name for dashing tom-cats. Rudolph Valentino was a handsome screen idol of the silent movie era who starred in romantic films like *The Sheik*.

VALMONT For seductive and aristocratic male cats. Valmont is the dangerously seductive aristocrat in Laclos' erotic novel *Dangerous Liaisons*.

VAN GOGH An artistic name for colourful tom-cats. Van Gogh was the Dutch post-Impressionist painter, famous for his striking picture *Sunflowers*.

VANILLA A spice-inspired name for sweet-natured female felines. Vanilla essence is used to flavour sweets and puddings.

VELVET   For soft-furred cats of either sex.

VENICE   An Italian name for water-loving tom-cats. The Italian city of Venice is built on over 100 islands.

VENUS   A mythical name for beautiful, amorous female felines. Venus was the Roman goddess of love.

VERDI   A music-inspired name for vocal tom-cats. Giuseppe Verdi was an Italian opera composer, whose works include *Rigoletto* and *La Traviata*.

VERMICELLI   A pasta-inspired name for slim cats of either sex. Vermicelli is a type of fine noodle.

VESPA   For speedy cats of either sex. The Vespa is a popular Italian motorbike.

VICTOR   A dashing name for warrior-like tom-cats. The name comes from the Latin for 'victorious'.

VICTORIA   For queenly female felines. Queen Victoria ruled over the United Kingdom between 1837 and 1901.

VIENNA A European name for cosmopolitan, coffee-coloured female felines. Vienna, the capital of Austria, is famous for its coffee-houses.

VIKING An appropriate name for ferocious tom-cats, especially suitable for ginger toms. The Vikings were Scandinavian sea warriors noted for their ferocity and their red hair.

VIKRAM A literary Indian name for intelligent male cats. Vikram Seth is a contemporary Indian novelist and poet, author of the best-selling novel *A Suitable Boy*.

VIOLA A music-inspired name for vocal female cats. The viola is a musical instrument of the violin family.

VIOLET A floral name for pretty female cats. The violet is a sweet-scented purple or white flower.

VIRAGO An appropriate name for strong-willed female cats. A virago is a woman of fighting spirit.

VIRGIL A literary name for thoughtful tom-cats. Virgil was a famous Roman poet, author of the *Aeneid*.

VISCONTI A film-inspired name for handsome, aristocratic tom-cats. Luchino Visconti was an aristocratic Italian film director, whose work includes *The Leopard* and *Death in Venice*.

VIVIEN A Hollywood name for glamorous green-eyed female felines. Vivien Leigh was the beautiful green-eyed actress who starred in the film epic *Gone With the Wind*.

VODKA A Russian name for spirited cats of either sex. Vodka is a colourless alcoholic drink with a distinctive flavour.

VULCAN A mythical name for fiery-tempered tom-cats. Vulcan was the Roman god of fire, patron of smiths and metalworkers.

WALDO   A literary name for nature-loving male cats. Ralph Waldo Emerson was an American essayist and poet, author of *Nature*.

WALNUT   A nutty name for brown-furred tom-cats.

WALRUS   For large, long-toothed tom-cats. The male walrus has large tusks for digging and fighting.

WALTER   A humorous name for dreamy male cats. American humorist James Thurber wrote *The Secret Life of Walter Mitty*, about an inveterate day-dreamer.

WARHOL   A pop art name for temperamental male cats. Andy Warhol was a famous experimental US pop artist and film-maker.

WARREN   A Hollywood name for dashingly good-looking

tom-cats. Handsome actor Warren Beatty starred in films like *Bonnie and Clyde*.

WASHINGTON   An American name for stately tom-cats. American general George Washington became the USA's first President and was noted for his statesmanship.

WATERCRESS   A plant-inspired name for water-loving cats of either sex. Watercress, with its peppery leaves, is cultivated in water.

WATSON   A literary name for stolid tom-cats. Doctor Watson was Sherlock Holmes's faithful sidekick, a foil for the detective's rapier-sharp mind.

WAVERLEY   A literary name for romantic male cats. *Waverley* is a famous novel by the popular author Sir Walter Scott.

WEBSTER   A literary name for dignified tom-cats immortalized by P. G. Wodehouse in *The Story of Webster*. Wodehouse wrote of Webster that he was 'large and very black and very composed'.

WELLINGTON   A distinguished name given to a black cat with white 'boots' markings. Arthur Wellington was a famous British general and statesman who gave his name to waterproof boots.

WESLEY   A religious name for devout male cats. John Wesley was the founder of Methodism.

WESTMINSTER   A parliamentary name for vocal male cats. The Palace of Westminster contains the British parliament, embodied by the House of Commons and the House of Lords and is noted for noisy debates.

WHISKERS   A classic name for cats of either sex with long whiskers.

WHISKY   A Scottish name for tawny-brown cats of either sex. The name comes from the Gaelic for 'water of life'.

WHITIE   A popular name for white cats of either sex.

WILBERFORCE   A distinguished name for generous male cats. William Wilberforce was a famous British philanthropist who led a successful campaign to abolish the British slave trade.

WILBY The name of a handsome, fine-furred Burmese tom of my acquaintance, named after his town of birth.

WILDE A literary name for dapper male cats. Oscar Wilde was a noted Victorian aesthete, dramatist and poet, author of the witty comedies *An Ideal Husband* and *The Importance of Being Earnest*.

WILLIAM An appropriate name for regal tom-cats. William the Conqueror defeated Harold II at the Battle of Hastings. The name became a recurring kingly one.

WILLOW A name for cats of either sex partial to tree-climbing. The willow is a graceful tree, usually found in wetlands.

WINDSOR A dignified name for regal male cats. Windsor has been Britain's royal family's name since 1917.

WINSTON A political name for tough, pugnacious tom-cats who enjoy battles. Sir Winston Churchill was the British statesman who became Prime Minister in 1940, during WWII, and was noted for his leadership qualities during wartime.

WISTERIA A flower-inspired name for graceful female felines. The wisteria is an ornamental twining vine.

WOODY A film-inspired name for neurotic male cats. Film director Woody Allen drew on his own insecure persona in films like *Annie Hall* and *Manhattan*.

WOOSTER A Wodehouse-inspired name suitable for dim-witted male cats. Bertie Wooster is the dim hero of P. G. Wodehouse's classic comic novels about Jeeves and Wooster.

WYNDHAM An old-fashioned name for male cats.

XENOPHON A Greek name for belligerent tom-cats. Xenophon was a Greek soldier and historian.

YAM A vegetable-inspired name for brown-furred cats of either sex. The yam is a brown-skinned, starchy tuber.

YASMIN An exotic-sounding name for beautiful female felines. Yasmin Le Bon is a leading fashion model.

YEHUDI A music-inspired name for elegant, vocal tom-cats. Sir Yehudi Menuhin is a world-famous violinist.

YVES A designer-inspired name for elegant male cats. Yves St Laurent is a French fashion designer noted for his stylish clothes.

ZACHARIAH   The distinguished name of the large, imposing
            black cat in Elizabeth Goudge's children's classic
            The Little White Horse.

ZAMBIA   An Africa-inspired name for sun-loving cats of
            either sex. Zambia is a central African country.

ZANZIBAR   A tropical name for fragrant cats of either sex.
            Zanzibar, an island off Tanzania, is noted for its
            cloves.

ZEN   A Buddhist name for serene cats of either sex,
            especially appropriate for oriental felines. Zen
            Buddhism emphasizes enlightenment from master
            to disciple and Transcendental Meditation.

ZENO   A Greek name for philosophical tom-cats. Zeno
            was a Greek philosopher noted for his paradoxes.

ZEUS   A mythological name for magnificent male cats. Zeus was the supreme Greek god who ruled over the Olympian deities.

ZIEGFELD   A showbiz name for flamboyant tom-cats. Florenz Ziegfeld was a famous American theatrical producer, famous for his lavish revue *The Ziegfeld Follies*.

ZOG   An Albanian name for regal tom-cats. Zog I was the King of Albania.

ZOLA   A literary name for thoughtful male cats. Emile Zola was a noted French novelist, the author of *Thérèse Raquin* and *Germinal*.

ZORBA A Greek name for carousing tom-cats. Zorba is the life-loving protagonist of the novel *Zorba the Greek* by Kazantzakis.

ZORRO A dashing name for daredevil male cats. Zorro is the mysterious masked hero in a popular TV series.

ZSA ZSA A glamorous name, especially suitable for long-haired female Persian cats, inspired by Hollywood actress Zsa Zsa Gabor.

ZUCCHERO An Italian name for sweet-natured cats of either sex. *Zucchero* is the Italian for 'sugar'.

ZULEIKA From the Arabic for 'pretty girl', a suitable name for attractive female felines. Zuleika Dobson was the fatally attractive heroine in Max Beerbohm's comic eponymous novel.

Twin or Couple Cat Names

APPLES AND PEARS   A fruity couple of names with cockney overtones.

BACON AND EGGS   A breakfast-inspired pair of names, good for early-rising felines.

BILL AND BEN   Simple, childhood names for a pair of cats inspired by the classic TV flowerpot men.

BONNIE AND CLYDE   Dashing names for an adventurous male–female partnership, inspired by the film about a young couple who embark on a life of crime.

BREAD AND BUTTER   A domestic, down-to-earth pair of names.

BUBBLE AND SQUEAK   A domestic pair of names, appropriate for squeaking kittens.

CASTOR AND POLLUX   Heavenly names for a pair of inseparable male cats. Castor and Pollux, heavenly twins, were turned into stars so as not to be separated.

DONNER AND BLITZEN   Dramatic Teutonic names for a pair of cats.

FORTNUM AND MASON Elegant English names for food-loving cats, inspired by the famous London grocer's on Piccadilly.

GIN AND TONIC A quintessentially English, drink-inspired pair of names.

GOG AND MAGOG For a pair of large, strong male cats. In British folklore Gog and Magog were a couple of giants.

HAM AND CHEESE A classic sandwich-inspired combination for greedy cats.

KIRK AND SPOCK The perfect names for cats belonging to Trekkies, inspired by *Star Trek*'s protagonists.

LAUREL AND HARDY The perfect names for a couple of comic cats. Stan Laurel and Oliver Hardy were a pair of thin and fat film comedians who enjoyed huge popularity.

LEMON AND LIME Citrus-inspired names for a yellow-eyed and green-eyed pair of cats, inspired by yellow lemons and green limes.

MARKS AND SPENCER A sensible pair of names inspired by the leading retailer.

MARX AND ENGELS The name given to a thoughtful pair of cats belonging to a friend of mine in pre-Thatcher days.

MORECAMBE AND WISE A classic combination for a pair of male comedians.

PEACHES AND CREAM Food-inspired names for a pair of luscious cats.

PINKY AND PERKY Comic names for a couple of cats, inspired by the puppet characters.

ROCK 'N' ROLL A music-inspired name for a pair of fun-loving cats.

ROMEO AND JULIET A romantic pair of names for a loving couple of cats.

ROMULUS AND REMUS Names inspired by classic Roman history for tough tom-cats. Romulus and Remus were the legendary founders of Rome, suckled by a she-wolf as babies.

RONNIE AND REGGIE A tough pair of tom-cat names inspired by the notorious East End gangsters the Kray Twins.

SALT AND PEPPER	The perfect names for a pair of black and white cats, inspired by the table condiments.
SAMSON AND DELILAH	For a strong-willed male and female pair. In the Bible Samson was a strong man, betrayed by his passionate mistress Delilah.
SAUSAGE AND MASH	Food-inspired names for a couple of greedy cats.
SENSE AND SENSIBILITY	A Jane Austen-inspired pair of names for a couple of female sibling cats. In her novel *Sense and Sensibility* Jane Austen explores the characters of two sisters: the romantic Marianne and the priggish Eleanor.
SOOTY AND SWEEP	Puppet-inspired names for an affectionate pair of cats.
SUGAR AND SPICE	A food-inspired pair of names for a couple of sweet-natured cats.
SYMI AND SYBI	Similar-sounding names, given to a pair of attractive black cats of my acquaintance.

VICTORIA AND ALBERT	A dignified and regal pairing, inspired by Queen Victoria and her beloved consort Prince Albert.
YIN AND YANG	A pair of names with oriental overtones, especially suitable for Siamese or Burmese. In Chinese thought yin and yang are the female and male universal principles.

Triplet Cat Names

ARAMIS, ATHOS AND PORTHOS	A debonair trio of names for swashbuckling tom-cats with a flair for fighting, the names of the three musketeers of Dumas' famous novel.
CHICO, GROUCHO AND HARPO	A trio of names for comic cats inspired by the wise-cracking comic film actors the Marx brothers, stars of classic film comedies like *Duck Soup*.
FAITH, HOPE AND CHARITY	Virtuous names for well-behaved female cats.
SHADRACH, MESHACH AND ABEDNEGO	A splendid trio of biblical names for courageous tom-cats with a penchant for heat.